LAW ENFORCEMENT
INTERPERSONAL COMMUNICATION
and CONFLICT MANAGEMENT
The IMPACT Model

This book is dedicated to my wife, Monica. Without her love and encouragement, this book would never have been possible.

LAW ENFORCEMENT INTERPERSONAL COMMUNICATION and CONFLICT MANAGEMENT
The IMPACT Model

Brian D. Fitch
Los Angeles County Sheriff's Department

Los Angeles | London | New Delhi
Singapore | Washington DC

Los Angeles | London | New Delhi
Singapore | Washington DC

FOR INFORMATION:

SAGE Publications, Inc.

2455 Teller Road

Thousand Oaks, California 91320

E-mail: order@sagepub.com

SAGE Publications Ltd.

1 Oliver's Yard

55 City Road

London EC1Y 1SP

United Kingdom

SAGE Publications India Pvt. Ltd.

B 1/I 1 Mohan Cooperative Industrial Area

Mathura Road, New Delhi 110 044

India

SAGE Publications Asia-Pacific Pte. Ltd.

3 Church Street

#10-04 Samsung Hub

Singapore 049483

Acquisitions Editor: Jerry Westby

Editorial Assistant: Laura Kirkhuff

Production Editor: Olivia Weber-Stenis

Copy Editor: Judy Selhorst

Typesetter: Hurix Systems Pvt.Ltd.

Proofreader: Christine Dahlin

Indexer: Molly Hall

Cover Designer: Candice Harman

Marketing Manager: Liz Thornton

Printed in the United States of America

ISBN 978-1-5063-0337-6

This book is printed on acid-free paper.

15 16 17 18 19 10 9 8 7 6 5 4 3 2 1

CONTENTS

FOREWORD

Randy Means

———•———

I learned early in my 35-year law enforcement career that human relations skills are important, but it was not until years later that I realized, profoundly for me, just how important they are. I learned also that maximizing performance in this area wasn't going to happen by itself in the natural flow of law enforcement affairs.

There are a number of factors working against that possibility. They begin with issues like age (young), gender (male), and associated subcultural influences—for example, the idea that being "nice" to people is a sign of weakness that will cause people to try to take advantage of you, and this will get you hurt or killed. Of course, the longer I work with law enforcement, the more veteran professionals I encounter who prove that it is possible to be "nice" and "tactical" at the same time, and that being "nice" *is* "tactical" most of the time. Actually, what's not "tactical" is fighting, which dramatically increases the risk of injury and death to both officers and citizens.

I learned that some officers can walk into a biker bar, make an arrest, and leave with a friend—not every time, certainly, but a lot of the time. I learned also that some officers can start a fight at a pacifist convention, and that those officers often have reputations in this regard. Other officers don't welcome their arrival at a call in progress because of their tendency to incite people and aggravate situations: "Everything was fine until *he* got here."

It turns out that in our world there are anger reducers and anger producers. These "bulls in a china shop" are, by their behaviors, anger producers. They are a danger to themselves and others and often seem to be unaware of it, blaming others for the negative outcomes of their encounters or sometimes reveling in them. In any event, these problem children need to be fixed or removed from law enforcement employment. They make everything worse and a great deal more dangerous for everyone. Their problems can get other officers hurt or killed.

Of course, these same officers also gum up criminal investigations and cause more complaints, lawsuits, and liability. Good officers end up the subjects of personnel complaints or lawsuits just for being where these anger producers are working. The more conflict there is in police transactions, the worse everything is for everybody.

A highly successful law enforcement veteran (and widely recognized interpersonal communication skills trainer) told me long ago that "voluntary compliance is the gold standard in law enforcement professionalism." He was of course talking about not having to fight people to get things done. My only refinement of that thought over the years since is to note that compliance involves doing what you're told. I refer to compliance as the silver standard. I believe that voluntary cooperation—what the law calls "voluntariness"—is the gold standard. When officers seek voluntary cooperation, people feel that they are making their own choices, not being bossed around, and that their freedom, particularly their freedom of choice, is not being stripped away. Through such practice, everybody involved tends to be reasonably happy and the law is almost never offended. In life and in the law, there is a profound and substantive difference between asking and telling.

Everyone knows that some officers are much better than others at getting a suspect to provide a voluntary confession. The same is true of orchestrating a legally voluntary citizen contact or getting a voluntary consent to search. Some officers are simply a lot better than others at getting voluntary cooperation. Obviously, they accomplish most of this superior law enforcement work through their exceptional human relations and interpersonal communication skills—they "kill people with kindness," or their gift of gab at least—and in this process further virtually all broader law enforcement interests.

The starting point, then, is simply to realize that the most important improvements in police effectiveness and professionalism are made largely through improvements in human relations and interpersonal communication skills. For all the technological advancements in policing, it remains a people profession. Many have suggested the applicability to law enforcement work of the Golden Rule found in religious teachings. Obviously, no single approach works every time, and being "nice" to people is not always possible or even wise in certain situations, but treating people with respect, dignity, and all the kindness that circumstances permit is usually a good start in public contact professionalism.

The author of this book, Brian D. Fitch, has more than 33 years of full-time service with the Los Angeles County Sheriff's Department; he has worked extensively in patrol, detention, and investigations, as well as in training at both his own department's academy and the Los Angeles Police Department Academy. He instructs law enforcement personnel nationally and internationally on communication, leadership, and ethics. He also holds faculty positions at California State University, Long Beach; Woodbury University; and Southwestern University School of Law. His master's degree in communication studies and his doctoral degree in human development complement his vast applied experience, making him one of only a handful of scholar-practitioners in the United States capable of authoring this exceptional book.

Law Enforcement Interpersonal Communication and Conflict Management: The IMPACT Model presents a plain-language statement of what law enforcement officers should do, and what their employers should require, in public contact professionalism. It should serve as a guide for professional standards organizationally. It provides a model—a guiding framework—for approaching this subject matter in real life and for enjoying the enormous advantages, both personal and professional, of "beneficial" communication. I believe that this book, along with Dale Carnegie's famous *How to Win Friends and Influence People*, should be required reading for all law enforcement officers.

PREFACE

Why This Book?

———•◦•———

Communication—the human connection—is the key to personal and career success.

—Paul J. Meyer

I have worked as a full-time law enforcement professional in Southern California for more than 33 years. In fact, I have spent the whole of my adult life in law enforcement. I have worked in jails, as a uniformed patrol officer, as an investigator, as a training officer, and as a supervisor. Regardless of my assignment, my successes and failures have always rested on my abilities to communicate and to connect with others. For nearly 20 years, I have studied, taught, and practiced the principles described in this book. I have also studied and observed (with great interest) the communication practices of thousands of officers—some successful, others not so much so. I have watched in admiration as talented officers have elicited confessions, calmed irate motorists, and "talked" bad guys to jail, all without so much as raising their voices. On the other hand, I have seen how an officer's words and body language can turn an otherwise positive contact into a messy, and often unnecessary, physical confrontation.

This book represents the total of everything I have learned, studied, and practiced over more than three decades on the job. It also reflects the sum of my formal education, advanced officer training, and the mentoring I have received from experts in the field. Other books on law enforcement communication are available, but most of them fall into one of two categories: those written by academicians, typically with no law enforcement experience or practical understanding; and those written by law enforcement officers, usually consisting of little more than collections of "war stories." The first type of book typically focuses exclusively on communication theory and research, offering little, if any, advice on how to "apply" those lessons in the "real world." The second type offers plenty of practical advice but fails to provide any coherent formula for how or when it should be applied, how to understand one's failures, and, most important, how to repeat one's successes.

What has been missing is a book that combines the theoretical with the practical in ways that enable officers to improve their communication skills by understanding how, why, and when to apply a number of simple, clearly defined principles. When it comes to communicating and connecting with irate, frustrated, and emotional people, happenstance is simply not good enough. Only by understanding both the "why" (theoretical) and the "when" (practical) can officers truly appreciate what they are doing right, what they are doing wrong, and how they can improve their future contacts. It is one thing to have successes (or failures)—it is another thing altogether to understand how to repeat those successes (or avoid those failures) with consistency and across a variety of contexts. The IMPACT principles described in this volume constitute a comprehensive and easy-to-understand model of communication that can be applied to virtually any type of encounter, because the principles that lead to successful criminal interviews apply equally well to other situations in which soothing strong emotions, building trust, and managing conflict are important.

This book is unique because it combines theory with practice from the perspective of a practicing law enforcement professional. It reflects not only 20 years of study but also more than 30 years of real-world experience. I understand both the theoretical side of the problem and the practical side of dealing with real people in real situations. While research and theory can be interesting, the first question on the minds of most law enforcement professionals is "So what?" For example, studies show that the areas of the brain responsible for logic are switched off when a person becomes emotionally charged. Okay, so what? If we understand that a person's logical brain is switched off when he is emotionally charged, we also understand why the person loses his ability to think rationally. A person whose ability to think logically has been suspended is at the mercy of the emotional brain. It is not possible to reason with that person successfully until his rational brain has been reengaged. As we shall see in Chapter 2, if we understand this, we can employ a variety of tools for managing the person's emotional response, reengaging the rational brain, and, in many cases, gaining voluntary cooperation. This is why each discussion of theory and research findings in this book is followed by specific suggestions for how officers can best apply those findings to improve their abilities to communicate and to connect with others, to soothe strong emotions, and to manage conflict.

It is important to note—as I will mention again in Chapter 1—that nothing in this book should be taken to suggest that officers should ever compromise their safety. However, one thing has become clear to me over the years: Angry people can be dangerous people. Each time an officer is able to "talk a person to jail" or "talk a person down," the safer it is for everyone. Whenever a person is angry enough to fight, the situation is bad for everyone involved, regardless of the outcome. Over the past several decades, the actions of law enforcement officers everywhere have come under increased scrutiny from the media, special-interest groups, and the courts. I have seen the careers of many promising officers cut short by physical encounters, even when the officers were able to avoid the limelight. While there will inevitably be times when force is required, the less frequently an officer finds it necessary to "put hands on" someone, the better it is for everyone—the officer, the suspect, and the community at large.

While dealing with irate, difficult, and emotional people is part of the job, it is my hope that the material in this book will help to make police officers safer and more effective in every aspect of their work. The IMPACT model was developed specifically to provide officers with a set of principles that are easy to understand and easy to apply. Simply put, the better educated we are about communicating and connecting with others, the easier our jobs will be. I hope you enjoy reading this book as much as I enjoyed writing it.

Brian D. Fitch
Los Angeles, California

SAGE was founded in 1965 by Sara Miller McCune to support the dissemination of usable knowledge by publishing innovative and high-quality research and teaching content. Today, we publish more than 850 journals, including those of more than 300 learned societies, more than 800 new books per year, and a growing range of library products including archives, data, case studies, reports, and video. SAGE remains majority-owned by our founder, and after Sara's lifetime will become owned by a charitable trust that secures our continued independence.

Los Angeles | London | New Delhi | Singapore | Washington DC

INTRODUCTION TO THE IMPACT
PRINCIPLES

———•◦•———

Communication works for those who work at it.

—John Powell

On the evening of September 21, 2010, Iraq War veteran Brock Savelkoul decided to end his life. Brock was one of more than 2 million troops who had deployed to Iraq since 2001. During his two deployments, Brock survived two bomb blasts. The first occurred early in his first tour; the second took place in January 2009, when an enemy rocket exploded near his trailer. The blasts left Brock the victim of both a concussion and traumatic brain injury, and the aftershocks left him struggling with a difficult mix of psychological and cognitive problems. Over time, Brock's behavior became increasingly bizarre. Eventually, he was picked up by U.S. embassy and military officials and admitted to Tripler Army Medical Center in Honolulu, where he was diagnosed as suffering from a psychotic breakdown. Brock was again admitted for treatment later in 2009, this time to Fort Riley Medical Center in Kansas. Doctors now labeled him as suffering from posttraumatic stress disorder (PTSD). In March 2010, Brock was honorably discharged from the army and placed on temporary disability due to PTSD. His military awards included the Purple Heart, the Army Commendation Medal, and the Army Achievement Medal.

Brock returned home to Minot, North Dakota, but his problems continued. He had trouble sleeping at night, often waking while thrashing his arms and legs. He even found himself panicked by the explosions at a local July 4 fireworks show. Brock struggled to regain control of his life. He wanted to continue his psychological treatments, but the nearest Veterans Administration Hospital was 271 miles from his home. By this time, Brock was unable to remember birthdays, anniversaries, or the date his mother died. Finally, it all became too much for him to bear. On the evening of September 21, Brock sent his father and sister a message: "I love you guys more than anything. Never forget it. I can't do this anymore." His father rushed to the family home, only to find another note from Brock: "No hope for me. Love you so much."

Brock armed himself with six guns—a DPMS AR-15, two hunting rifles, and three handguns—and several hundred rounds of ammunition. The next time anyone heard from Brock was around 6:20 p.m., when he walked into a convenience store about 120 miles west of Minot and pointed a rifle at one of the patrons. "Do you want to die?" Brock asked before fleeing the store. A Watford City police officer responded to the scene. The officer spotted Brock's vehicle a short time later and activated his vehicle's lights and siren. Rather than pulling over, Brock sped up, ultimately reaching speeds of 105 miles per hour. He continued down the highway, across the river, and toward the North Dakota badlands.

Back home, Brock's father and sister had told a friend from the local police department about Brock's past, that he was a veteran suffering from PTSD and heavily armed. The friend relayed the information to the police.

Eventually, Brock's truck ran out of gas. He pulled over on a farm road. Within seconds, he was surrounded by sheriff's deputies, police officers, and highway patrol troopers. "Drop the gun," the officers yelled. "Drop the gun." Over the next two hours, Brock engaged in a tense standoff with law enforcement. He paced, smoked, brandished weapons, and even went so far as to fire a round into his truck. At one point, Brock walked within a few feet of a patrol car, raised a 9 mm handgun to his side, and yelled, "Go ahead, shoot me!" But the officers, demonstrating tremendous discipline, held their fire.

Throughout the incident, Megan Christopher, a junior officer with no real training or experience in crisis negotiation, talked to Brock non-stop. She tried to put herself in Brock's shoes and to empathize with the former staff sergeant. She worked to identify what Brock was feeling and thinking, listened carefully to his concerns, and monitored her words. As Trooper Christopher remained safely behind the door of her patrol car in the cold, the rain, and the sleet, she never stopped talking. Finally, she said, "Brock, I'd like to meet you. Please put the gun down so we can meet."

At around 9:30 p.m., more than three hours after the incident began, Brock fired his gun into an open field. Christopher promised to give Brock a cell phone if he put down his weapon. Brock laid his gun on the ground in front of him. The trooper walked toward Brock holding the cell phone. As Brock turned to face her, another trooper, fearing that Brock was spinning to attack, fired a Taser. Brock stiffened, fell to the ground, and was quickly handcuffed by officers. When it was all over, Christopher knelt down next to Brock, put her hand to his cheek, and said, "I'm Megan. I'm glad to meet you."

INTERPERSONAL COMMUNICATION IN LAW ENFORCEMENT

It is impossible to say what might have happened that evening if Trooper Christopher had failed to pick up the public address microphone in her cruiser and start a dialogue with Brock. Certainly, all of the law enforcement professionals on scene that day demonstrated exemplary discipline and courage. Nonetheless, it was Trooper Christopher's abilities to identify and manage emotions, listen actively, promote positive behavior, build rapport, control her response, and empathize with Brock that helped bring about a peaceful resolution to what might have otherwise been another statistical tragedy.

All law enforcement officers have one thing in common: We are in the problem-solving business. People don't call the police when everyone is at their best. They request our assistance when someone is hostile, angry, frustrated, aggressive, intoxicated or under the influence of drugs, or emotionally or psychologically disturbed. In other words, people request law enforcement's assistance only when someone is at his worst, when he has lost his ability to think logically about his behaviors or the consequences of his actions. To make matters worse, many of the people we contact have histories of violence. As any veteran officer can testify, there is no such thing as a "routine" call for service. Every call and every contact has the potential for violence. Fortunately, criminal justice professionals throughout the nation are very good at managing people in crisis. While this is hardly news to anyone serving in law enforcement, it has only recently been validated empirically. A survey conducted by the International Association of Chiefs of Police (2001) found that less than 1% of all calls for service result in a use of force. Rather, officers are able to gain compliance by demonstrating command presence, building rapport, and communicating effectively.

As Trooper Christopher's encounter with Brock illustrates, officers' abilities to connect and to communicate effectively are critical to their success in virtually every aspect of law enforcement. Officers' success at everything from vehicle stops to homicide investigations hinges on effective communication. Yet many officers fail to recognize the impact of their words and behaviors on others. To complicate matters further, few law enforcement agencies offer comprehensive training in communication skills, emotional management, and conflict resolution.

Even those officers who understand the importance of communication often dread the idea of attending a course on interpersonal skills. Being lectured on the value of nonverbal communication and practicing listening drills are not high on the "to do" lists of most officers. Most criminal justice professionals are doers. They believe that learning is best accomplished on the job. Law enforcement officers interact with peers, supervisors, victims, witnesses, subjects, and other members of the public on a daily basis, and many officers operate under the assumption that communication skills are something they develop naturally during the course of their normal job experience, without the need for special training. While it is certainly true that officers acquire a number of unique and valuable skills during the course of their daily activities, there is always room for improvement, even among the most expert communicators. It can also be argued that while many officers function competently in the absence of formal training, they never realize their full potential as communicators.

Regardless of how skilled, or unskilled, an officer may be, with the right attitude and process, everyone can learn to connect and to communicate with others more effectively. By building the right process, any officer has the potential to calm even the most irate, frustrated, or difficult person. Every law enforcement encounter consists of both process and outcome. The outcome is our goal, what we hope to accomplish. It may be calming an emotionally distraught motorist, reassuring an irate citizen, or convincing a suspect to surrender peacefully. The process consists of the tactics, strategies, and behaviors that we use to accomplish our goal. Too often, we focus only on achieving a particular outcome while overlooking the importance of process. Rather than concern ourselves with the long-term outcomes of good process, we emphasize the short-term benefits of satisfying our immediate needs. This approach, however, is shortsighted. The simple truth is that process matters.

Anytime we can create good process, we are more likely to get more of what we want—and less of what we don't want. Creating a successful process is not always easy, especially when time and resources are limited by staffing shortages, unfinished reports, and pending calls for service. Good process requires listening, patience, and empathy. And, while taking the time necessary to create good process might not always be the shortest distance between two points, in almost every case it will dramatically improve our chances of soothing strong emotions, resolving conflict, and gaining voluntary compliance.

BENEFITS OF EFFECTIVE INTERPERSONAL COMMUNICATION

The abilities to communicate and to connect with others have meaningful impacts on virtually every aspect of law enforcement. For those officers who are willing to invest the time and effort, better interpersonal effectiveness offers a number of advantages, including improved officer safety, heightened investigative awareness, fewer complaints and lawsuits, career advancement and recognition, better relationships (both on and off the job), and decreased stress and anxiety.

Improved Officer Safety

The abilities to communicate and to connect are vital officer safety skills. Angry, hostile, and emotionally distraught people can be dangerous people. By learning to recognize the messages that others are sending, officers are better able to detect and evaluate strong emotions before they spiral out of control. Similarly, by better understanding and monitoring their own words and behaviors, officers can avoid the hostilities that may arise when they unintentionally send the wrong signals. Officers are often unaware of how even the simplest behaviors can escalate a contact into a physical confrontation. Learning to pay attention to the behaviors of others, as well as to monitor their own words and actions, is an important step toward better officer safety.

Heightened Investigative Effectiveness

Good investigators recognize the importance of communicating and connecting with victims, witnesses, and subjects. They understand better than most the significance of building rapport, listening actively, and reading nonverbal behaviors. Good investigators realize that everything they do and say has important consequences. They realize that obtaining confessions, closing cases, and improving the safety of the communities they serve can be accomplished only through communication. In addition to being tactically sound, familiar with case law, and physically fit, interpersonal skills are among the most important abilities that any criminal justice professional can possess.

Fewer Complaints and Lawsuits

Regardless of the agency, location, or demographics, the most frequent complaint against officers involves "discourtesy." Time after time, it is not what officers say but how they say it that people find offensive. Complaints and lawsuits against officers and their agencies have been on the rise for years—a trend that shows no sign of slowing. In short, perceptions matter. While many of these complaints may be unfounded, the simple truth of the matter is that complaints, even merit-less complaints, can damage an officer's reputation, career, and promo-tional opportunities. One way that officers can reduce complaints is by better monitoring and managing their words and behaviors. The more skilled officers are at managing perceptions, the better their chances of avoiding frivolous complaints and lawsuits.

Career Recognition and Advancement

Regardless of officers' job knowledge or experience, they must be able to work well with others if they are to have any hope of recognition or advancement. When given a choice between two employees, one who is a "competent cop" but skilled with people and a second who is an "outstanding cop" but lacks interpersonal skills, most supervisors and managers will opt for the former. This is because few supervisors and managers want to work with officers who cannot communicate effec-tively, empathize with others, or manage their own emotions. This is especially true in specialized units, where one "difficult" personality can create an uncomfortable environment for everyone. Interpersonal skills have a greater impact on career opportunities than many officers realize. The better officers are at monitoring and managing their behaviors, at communicating, and at connecting with others, the better their chances of recognition and advancement.

Better Relationships

We rely on interpersonal skills to develop and maintain our personal and professional relationships. The relationships that we develop with the significant people in our lives are important to all of us. Our rela-tionships help us celebrate our victories and overcome our defeats, and they give us something and someone to look forward to at the end of the day. Officers who have poor interpersonal skills—those who, for exam-ple, are unable to recognize or manage emotions, are poor listeners, and have low empathy—can find it difficult to build lasting relationships, both on and off the job. The better officers are at communicating and connecting with others, the more successful they can be at developing and maintaining the important relationships in their lives.

Decreased Stress and Anxiety

Law enforcement, like life in general, is full of stressors. Traffic, bills, kids, supervisors, illness, taxes—all create stress and anxiety. The inability to communicate or to control emotions can add unnecessary feelings of stress and anxiety. Officers who have received a number of frivolous complaints, been passed over for opportunities, or have difficulty developing and maintaining relationships can suffer from the psychological, physical, and emotional effects of stress and anxiety. Building and maintaining important relationships, receiving deserved recognition, and avoiding frivolous lawsuits can significantly improve the quality of officers' personal and professional lives while reducing or, in some cases, eliminating unnecessary stress and anxiety.

COMMUNICATION MYTHS

While the ability to communicate with others effectively is a critical law enforcement skill, communication is not capable of solving every problem. The idea that talking more will always make things better is one of several common myths. In many cases, people understand each other just fine—they simply disagree. Their disagreement may center on values, beliefs, cultural issues, assumptions, or experiences. Officers often accept myth over truth because they do not know the difference. To make the most of our interpersonal skills, we must first understand what we can and cannot accomplish using communication.

Myth 1: Logic Makes Communication More Effective

While we like to think of ourselves as rational, analytical beings who make decisions based solely on logic, this is simply not the case. As the eminent psychologist Donald Hebb (1949) observed, man is the most emotional of all animals. Effective communicators recognize that every decision they make and every action they take is somehow influenced by emotion. Problems often occur when we forget the importance of emotion and focus instead on constructing logical arguments. Effective communicators look beyond words and logic to focus on emotion. They recognize that persuasion is not a logical process but an emotional one, and they construct their messages accordingly.

Myth 2: Learning Communication Makes You a Better Communicator

It is not true that learning communication will make someone a better communicator. There is a difference between knowledge and application. Understanding how to communicate is only part of the equation. Learning the skills and attitudes necessary to be an effective communicator can make a person a better communicator only when that learning is grounded in behavioral change. To be truly effective, the person must be willing and able to perform the required skills. Knowing what to do is not much help unless that knowledge is put to work. This is not the same thing as performing a new skill perfectly the first time out. Improving interpersonal skills is a process, not a destination. It takes knowledge, practice, and feedback for an individual to become a truly effective communicator.

Myth 3: Communication Is a One-Way Process

People not only send messages but also receive signals in the form of feedback. Feedback provides information about the receiver's reaction to the message in ways that allow the sender to correct inaccuracies, clarify perceptions, and adjust subsequent messages for the best response. Feedback can be verbal, nonverbal, or both. To use feedback effectively, the person sending the message must observe and interpret the receiver's reactions immediately following the message, especially nonverbal cues, such as shifts in voice tone, posture, eye contact, gestures, and facial expressions. Effective communicators understand the importance of feedback, monitor the reactions of others, and adjust or modify their behaviors to send the most accurate messages possible.

Myth 4: The Message Sent Is the Message Received

People often assume that the meaning of a message is "out there," that it exists independent of the parties sending and receiving the communication. The processes through which people construct and interpret messages, however, are uniquely personal, varying widely among individuals. We all interpret messages in light of our own expectations, assumptions, beliefs, values, goals, and experiences. As a result, in our decoding of messages we may not receive the intended meanings of the senders. Arguably, the most difficult part of communication is ensuring that the message sent is the message received. Learning to anticipate differences in perception while crafting the most effective messages possible represents the very foundation of successful communication.

Myth 5: You Can Refrain From Communicating

Many people assume that they can avoid communicating with someone simply by ignoring the person. However, we communicate continuously whenever we are in the presence of others. While some of our messages are intentional—that is, meant to transmit information or feelings, invoke a response, or both—we may send other messages without conscious awareness or intent. Regardless of our objective, every message contains important information about our thoughts, feelings, and attitudes. For example, facial expressions, gestures, and posture can all transmit subtle signs of interest, boredom, impatience, anger, or disgust without our conscious awareness that we are sending such messages and without our awareness of their effects. Effective communicators are self-aware. They understand that they communicate anytime they are in the presence of others and manage their behaviors appropriately.

Myth 6: Meaning Is Conveyed Only in Words

Perhaps the biggest mistake that communicators make is assuming that messages are contained only in the words they use. We react not to the words people use but to the meanings we ascribe to those words. The meanings that we assign are affected by our culture, experiences, values, beliefs, and expectations. The ways we interpret messages are also influenced by the context in which the communication occurs. Indeed, the meanings that we assign to messages can vary widely from one situation to the next. For example, a supervisor discussing an officer's performance with that officer in a formal setting (in the supervisor's office) can send a message that is different from that sent when the same issue is discussed in an informal setting (in the field over a cup of coffee). In fact, even the slightest change in context (for instance, where the supervisor and officer sit in relation to each other) can alter the ways messages are received and understood.

Myth 7: Good Communicators Are Born, Not Made

The idea that good communicators are born, not made, is grounded in the belief that to be an effective communicator, a person must be extroverted, social, and outgoing. In contrast, people with more reserved personalities are often viewed as less effective at connecting with others. While certain people seem to be naturally gifted at relating to others, anyone, regardless of personality or temperament, can learn to communicate more effectively. Communication is a skill and, like other skills, can be improved with the right combination of study and practice. While officers with reserved personalities may never feel as comfortable interacting with others as do their colleagues with naturally outgoing temperaments, they can still improve their interpersonal abilities in a number of areas. For example, officers' abilities to recognize emotions, listen effectively, and resolve conflict can all be improved with time, training, and practice.

THE IMPACT PRINCIPLES

While every encounter is unique, officers' abilities to motivate and to persuade depend to a large extent on their interpersonal effectiveness. One element that separates effective officers from their less effective counterparts is their purpose. Communicating and connecting with others begins with a clearly articulated plan. Arguably, many of the communication breakdowns that take place between officers and others occur because the officers approach the exchanges with no clear plan or purpose. While many law enforcement agencies require officers to attend some form of communication or human relations training, no standardized, systematic model of interpersonal skills has been available to help officers manage the myriad interpersonal challenges they encounter on a daily basis. As a result, officers are often unsure how best to overcome strong emotions, resolve conflict, and manage irate, frustrated, or difficult people.

The IMPACT model was designed specifically to provide law enforcement professionals with a systematic, easy-to-follow model of interpersonal communication and conflict management skills that can be applied to virtually any type of law enforcement contact. The IMPACT model focuses on building successful process. As stated earlier, process matters. If we build the right process, we will be more successful at connecting and communicating with others, avoiding unnecessary hostilities and frivolous complaints, and getting more of what we need. The model is built around six core principles:

- Identify and manage emotions.
- Master the story.
- Promote positive behavior.
- Achieve rapport.
- Control your response.
- Take perspective.

While the use of all these principles is critical to officers' dealing effectively with difficult or angry people, managing conflict, motivating others, and solving problems, the order of their application may vary. Every law enforcement contact is unique. An officer may find it helpful to begin with the first principle (identify and manage emotions) and work methodically through the model in one instance, but may discover it is more effective to begin with, for example, the fifth principle (control your response) before reverting to the second (master the story) on another occasion. Similarly, in one case an officer may find it necessary to work through all six steps, while only two steps may be required during a different contact. And while the principles that officers select and the order in which they are applied may vary according to the unique demands of particular situations, the core principles of the IMPACT model remain constant.

Identify and Manage Emotions

Trooper Christopher recognized Brock's emotional distress early in the encounter described at the beginning of this chapter. In police work, it is not a question of whether strong emotions will emerge; rather, it is a question of how they can best be handled when they do. Strong emotional responses occur when the emotional parts of the brain (limbic system) override the rational, thinking areas (neocortex). Strong emotions make it difficult—in some cases impossible—for people to think logically about their behaviors or the consequences of their actions. Before we can expect a person who is experiencing strong emotions to think or act logically, we must first identify and manage those emotions. To whatever extent we can decrease the emotional arousal, we should see a corresponding increase in the person's abilities to listen and to reason.

Three of the most effective tools for managing strong emotions are asking questions, reframing, and paraphrasing. The first of these, asking questions, requires the person to pause and to reflect—in other words, to think. While answering questions might not seem to be a difficult task, it requires deliberate mental focus. It also forces the person to engage the rational, thinking areas of the brain. The second tactic, reframing, involves describing the problem while eliminating emotionally charged language. Reframing allows us to acknowledge a person's feelings and concerns and to communicate that his problem matters without making a bad situation worse. Additionally, it provides us with opportunities to model the kinds of language and behaviors that will best facilitate positive, meaningful dialogue. Trooper Christopher used reframing to acknowledge Brock's concerns while demonstrating the behaviors she wanted him to adopt, such as a calm voice and relaxed demeanor.

The final method, paraphrasing, is a way of acknowledging or demonstrating that we have been listening. Paraphrasing is a simple yet powerful tool for acknowledging a person's concerns, checking for understanding, and correcting any confusion. It also provides a unique opportunity for the person to listen to his own words, a process that can eliminate the person's need to repeat the same message multiple times in the hope of "finally getting through" to someone who cares. Despite the simplicity of this approach, acknowledging and validating a person's feelings and concerns is an important step toward better communication, conflict management, and problem solving.

Master the Story

Understanding Brock's needs and fears required Trooper Christopher to listen carefully. Mastering another person's story is not always as simple as it might appear. In Trooper Christopher's case, it began with a genuine desire and willingness to understand the situation from Brock's perspective. Too often, we assume that those who are behaving badly are doing so because they are "bad" people. In reality, there may be any number of hidden factors influencing people's behavior. It's easy for us to blame others when we don't understand their feelings, motives, and intentions. Listening actively, asking questions, and taking a genuine interest in the other person allows us to better understand the story from her perspective. The better we understand the person and her story, the better our chances of offering a solution.

Listening actively requires that we listen beyond the words a person uses. People communicate information and feelings using both verbal and nonverbal cues. Verbal communication consists of the words used to transmit information, while nonverbal communication comprises those parts of the message sent without words. Facial expressions, gestures, eye contact, posture, and physical appearance all convey important information about a person's attitudes, thoughts, and emotions. However, the precise meaning of what a person is thinking or feeling usually depends on both verbal and nonverbal messages, not on either type in isolation.

Mastering the story requires that we suspend our assumptions, ask questions, and listen carefully to the person's answers. It also requires that we pay attention to new information, especially when it contradicts our assumptions—something that is not always easy to do. As noted previously, however, all law enforcement professionals are in the problem-solving business. An officer who is annoyed by a stream of complaining people is akin to a physician who is irritated by a long line of sick patients. In the same way that good physicians ask questions and gather information before making a diagnosis, good officers recognize the importance of understanding both the person and her problem before offering a solution.

Promote Positive Behavior

One of the most challenging aspects of Trooper Christopher's encounter with Brock was how the trooper could best promote positive behavior. Motivating and persuading others begins with the idea that all humans share a number of basic needs, including the needs to feel safe and in control of our lives. Because these needs are so fundamental, people often go to great lengths to protect them. When people feel threatened or controlled, they often act in negative, aggressive, and, in some cases, violent ways to reestablish a sense of safety and self-determination. One way of allowing a person to retain a sense of control is to offer choices. In other words, allow the person to believe that something was his own idea or decision.

A second way that we can help people feel safe is by reducing uncertainty. We can best accomplish this by providing them with explanations of our decisions and actions, as well as advice about what to expect. The criminal justice system can be intimidating, especially for people who have never been exposed to its many (sometimes subtle) complexities. Most people know little, if anything, about the policies, procedures, and laws that most officers take for granted. As an old adage suggests, people usually do better with the "what" if they understand the "why."

In addition to the need for safety, most people are fiercely independent. Research has consistently supported the folk notion of "reverse psychology"; that is, the idea that people react strongly against attempts to limit their freedom of choice. Generally speaking, whenever we restrict a person's freedom, three consequences result: (a) The person wants to perform the forbidden action, (b) the person takes steps to reclaim the lost freedom, and (c) the person has negative feelings toward the individual who restricted her choices. Officers who understand the human need for control can use it to their benefit by allowing people to feel as if they are making voluntary decisions to cooperate or comply, whether or not such choices actually exist.

Achieve Rapport

Trooper Christopher had to work especially hard that evening to achieve a sense of rapport with Brock. Nevertheless, she recognized that developing and maintaining rapport was critical. The better we are at establishing and maintaining rapport, the more successful we are in connecting, motivating, and gaining voluntary compliance. Too often, we react impulsively to difficult situations and people. When confronted with a demanding person, for example, many officers either strike back ("fight fire with fire") or break off contact altogether. In the first case, if someone is rude or stubborn, the officer responds in kind by providing the person with a "dose of his own medicine." In the second case, rather than attempting to work through any differences, the officer simply walks away, beating a hasty retreat and avoiding the encounter altogether. While these techniques can be effective in a limited sense, they tend to stifle communication, discourage rapport, and undermine cooperation.

One of the most time-tested ways of achieving rapport is to make the other person feel special. It is the need to feel special (important, successful) that motivates people to drive expensive cars, wear designer clothes, and buy homes that are much larger than they really need. In his classic book *How to Win Friends and Influence People*, Dale Carnegie (1936/1981) notes that most people are filled with ego, and "history sparkles with amusing examples of famous people struggling for a feeling of importance" (p. 20). Rather than challenging a person's ego, we can increase our influence by focusing on our own credibility, likability, and power. This includes asking questions rather than demanding cooperation, complimenting rather than criticizing, and apologizing for any inconvenience, as appropriate.

The second facet of building rapport is communication. We communicate continuously whenever we are in the presence of others. Sending the right verbal, vocal, and visual messages is critical to our abilities to communicate and to connect with others. Our facial expressions, eye contact, posture, mannerisms, tone of voice, and words can all help to establish and maintain rapport. On the other hand, the wrong words, behaviors, or tone of voice can make an already bad situation worse. It is worth noting that we achieve our greatest impact on others when our verbal and nonverbal cues are consistent—that is, when our words and behaviors communicate the same message. The reverse is also true: If our words say one thing but our body language sends a different signal, people are less likely to trust our message. This is because people see nonverbal behaviors as accurate indicators of our true attitudes and feelings.

Control Your Response

Trooper Christopher realized that in addition to managing Brock's emotions, she needed to control her own response. Anytime we "lose it," we are a danger to ourselves and to others. The first step in controlling our emotional response is to recognize that each problem really consists of two issues: one practical, the other emotional. The practical issue is the topic or subject of concern, such as gaining the cooperation of a difficult motorist or taking a combative subject into custody. The emotional issue consists of our affective response to the practical problem, such as anger, frustration, or fear. Our inability to separate practical issues from emotional ones can create a host of problems, including stifling cooperation, impeding communication, and reducing our problem-solving effectiveness.

Next, we must work to identify our "hot buttons"—that is, the types of comments or actions by others that lead us to anger. Everyone has hot buttons, and part of managing our emotions effectively is recognizing our triggers. If we understand what upsets us, we will be better prepared when someone inevitably pushes our buttons. One way to prepare is to visualize a difficult encounter along with the proper response. This allows us to mentally prepare, or to "rehearse," in advance. Practicing correct responses, even if only in our minds, can help reduce our chances of becoming overly emotional when it matters most.

A third way to gain control of our emotions is to pay close attention to our choice of words. Some cognitive psychologists believe that the words and language we choose have a lot to do with how we respond emotionally. We constantly talk to ourselves, or engage in "self-talk," about the people, events, and things we encounter. The words we choose in our self-talk can either aggravate or mitigate our emotional responses. In fact, the language we use to describe events is believed to be one of the reasons that different people respond in different ways to the same events. Rather than using strong, emotional language to describe our feelings—for example, "This guy is a real idiot"—we should choose language with a cooler emotional tone, such as "This guy must be having a bad day."

Take Perspective

Trooper Christopher instinctively recognized the power of seeing the standoff from Brock's perspective. She tried to understand the emotional and psychological difficulties that Brock was experiencing—many of which were beyond his control—and how those challenges were influencing his behaviors. She also realized that there are as many different ways to see and to experience the same event as there are people involved. Too often, we assume that others think as we think, see the world as we see it, and should behave in the same ways that we would behave given a similar set of circumstances.

In simplest terms, the better we understand the other person's perspective, the better our chances of communicating and connecting. Understanding another's perspective begins with our acknowledgment of our own assumptions and biases. Arguably the single greatest barrier to our understanding others is our tendency to believe that we see the world as it really is, and that others should share our view. Our worldviews, beliefs, and assumptions are important because they influence the ways we label others. If we label someone "a problem," we will treat him accordingly. In contrast, if we label someone "a person with a problem," our interaction will look very different. It is difficult to overstate the importance of this distinction, because the labels we choose influence not only how we treat others but also how they treat us. If we believe a person is rude, and we treat her accordingly, the person will no doubt behave in ways consistent with our label—that is, she will behave rudely. When the person reacts to our label, it confirms our earlier belief, producing a spiral of discourteous behavior that eventually makes meaningful communication impossible.

One of the most effective ways to increase our influence is to see things from the other person's perspective. The better we understand the other person and his problem, the more our influence grows, often allowing us to gain cooperation in situations where we previously had little control. The importance of open-mindedness, tolerance, and empathy in law enforcement cannot be overstated, especially in the United States, which has arguably the most ethnically diverse populace in the world. Many U.S. cities are home to some of the largest ethnic populations outside their native countries. American law enforcement officers interact almost continuously with people whose cultural backgrounds, beliefs, customs, traditions, and norms are different from the officers' own. Indeed, with the United States becoming increasingly diverse, open-mindedness, tolerance, and the ability to see things from different perspectives are fast becoming the cornerstones of 21st-century law enforcement.

SUMMARY

The abilities to communicate and to connect with others are arguably the most important skills that any officer can possess. Indeed, communication skills are critical to officers' success in virtually every aspect of law enforcement. Although interpersonal skills are not a panacea, they can benefit officers in several important areas, including better officer safety, fewer complaints and lawsuits, and improved investigative effectiveness. However, despite the importance of communication, few law enforcement agencies offer comprehensive training in dealing with difficult people, managing emotions, and resolving conflict.

The IMPACT principles offer law enforcement professionals a systematic model for improving their communication and emotional management skills. The IMPACT model is based on the idea that process matters. Anytime we can build good process, we will be more successful at connecting and communicating with others, avoiding unnecessary hostilities and frivolous complaints, and getting more of what we need. Although the model is described in linear fashion, the IMPACT principles are not necessarily sequential, and officers are not limited in how they apply the model. What is important is the simultaneous interplay of the six core principles. Anytime officers encounter irate, frustrated, or difficult people, they will, in all likelihood, engage in several steps of the process simultaneously. For example, an officer may find it necessary to identify and manage the person's emotions, control his own response, and master the story while simultaneously promoting positive behavior and taking perspective. Regardless of their order of appearance, the IMPACT principles offer law enforcement professionals a valuable tool for managing difficult, irate, and frustrated people; improving officer safety; and improving communicative effectiveness.

At this point it is worth noting that nothing in this book should be taken to suggest that officers should ever compromise their tactics or safety. Before using any of the IMPACT principles, officers must first ensure their own safety and the safety of others. Proper use of the IMPACT model is grounded in appropriate tactics and discipline. Each year, thousands of law enforcement officers in the United States, as well as throughout the world, are victims of violent assault. Each year in the United States alone, dozens of officers are killed in the line of duty. Communication, although a vital tactic and critical to all officers' success, will not solve every law enforcement problem.

Each of the next six chapters outlines one of the IMPACT principles in greater detail, with Chapter 2 addressing the first: Identify and manage emotions. The book concludes with suggestions for improving communication competence.

STUDY QUESTIONS

1. According to the findings of the 2001 survey conducted by the International Association of Chiefs of Police, what percentage of calls for service result in a use of force?

2. Why are the abilities to communicate and to connect with others important law enforcement skills?

3. Describe three advantages of effective communication for law enforcement professionals.

4. What are four common myths about communication?

5. List the core principles of the IMPACT model.

6. What do you believe to be the most important principle in the model?

⊰ 2 ⊱

IDENTIFY AND MANAGE EMOTIONS

———•—•—

*The emotions aren't always immediately subject to reason, but they
are always immediately subject to action.*

—William James

We all experience an assortment of emotions every day. Joy, fear,
surprise, anger, disgust, and other feelings are such a fact of life
that we seldom stop to think about what they mean, how they occur,
or why they occur. When managed properly, emotions can enhance
our motivation, improve our relationships, and protect us from danger. When handled improperly, however, emotions can destroy careers,
damage relationships, and stifle our abilities to communicate and to
connect with others.

Emotions are complex feeling states that produce a host of cognitive, physiological, and behavioral changes. Cognitively, we experience
emotions as a shift in focus as our attention becomes fixed on a person
or object. Physiologically, we undergo a number of bodily changes,
including accelerated heart rate, elevated body temperature, accelerated breathing, dilated pupils, and muscular tension. Behaviorally, we
experience emotions as an impulse to act—that is, to move toward or
away from a person or object, a response commonly described as "fight
or flight."

Emotions do not occur in a vacuum. They have specific causes. We are angry with someone or about something. Indeed, it is the all-consuming focus of emotions that makes them so difficult to ignore. This seems especially true for anger, which can range in intensity from mild irritation to full-blown rage. Because emotions urge us to do something and do it quickly, they often create more problems than they solve. This has led some philosophers to conclude that before we can live a happy and fulfilled life, we must first learn to subjugate our emotions to the cold logic of reason.

HISTORY AND THE STUDY OF EMOTIONS

The Greek Stoics of the early third century B.C. believed that the "passions" do little more than cloud one's ability to reason. The Stoics taught that emotions, which result from errors in judgment, are something to be controlled. They further believed that a "sage" person of "moral and intellectual perfection" would not suffer the defect of emotions. Several centuries later, the French philosopher René Descartes proposed a "duality" of mind and body. Descartes suggested that the mind is completely separate from the body, an immaterial "thinking thing" driven by pure logic and void of self-defeating emotions. Logic and emotion, he maintained, are isolated processes, occurring in separate spheres—one in the mind, the other in the body. Descartes did not deny the existence of emotions; rather, he believed that rational thinking is unaffected by feelings. However, despite the long-standing popularity of these approaches, their authors could not have been more wrong.

Every decision that we make and every action that we take—from selecting which car to buy to deciding whom to marry—is somehow influenced by emotion. Because of the way we value logic in Western society, we are naturally inclined to view ourselves as rational and decision making as a purely logical pursuit. We observe and assess, identify our options, and choose the most logical course of action. Recent scientific evidence, however, suggests that our decisions and actions are heavily influenced by emotion. On one hand, we use logic to analyze data and assess outcomes. On the other hand, we rely on emotions to provide visceral feedback, intuitive insights, and "gut feelings." It seems that rather than simply weighing the logical costs and benefits of a decision, we use emotions to guide our choices and then engage in a post hoc search for reasons to justify our actions. The better we understand how and why emotions occur, the more effective we will be at soothing hurt feelings, managing conflict, and dealing with irate, frustrated, and difficult people.

Functions of Emotions

In addition to their role in problem solving and decision making, emotions serve a number of other important functions, including protection, attention, motivation, bonding, and communication.

- *Protection:* The primary purpose of our nervous system is to keep us alive. In simplest terms, the faster we respond to potential threats, the greater our chances of survival. Emotions have evolved as the primary way of alerting us to the presence of danger. At the first sign of threat, the emotional centers of the brain activate the body's stress response, sending signals to other areas of the brain and body to prime us for immediate action.

- *Attention:* Emotions affect what we notice, what we process, and what we remember. Negative emotions like fear and anger make it difficult for us to concentrate or remember, while positive emotions can generate energy and attention as well as enhance memory and recall.

- *Motivation:* Emotions are the driving forces that compel us to act. The things that motivate us are generally the same things that move us emotionally. The positive feelings we experience when we achieve personal goals motivate us to pursue other ambitions. Conversely, the negative emotions that follow a disappointment deter us from performing certain behaviors.

- *Bonding:* Emotions make it possible for us to form important relationships and to bond with others. The bond that a parent shares with a child and the connection between a husband and wife are simply not possible without emotions.

- *Communication:* We use our emotions to initiate and to regulate social interaction with others, as well as to reinforce or to modify other aspects of our communication. We do so through our facial expressions, posture, eye contact, and bodily movement—all of which provide important clues about our thoughts, feelings, and attitudes.

While emotions perform a number of necessary and important functions, an inability to recognize and to control emotions can create a host of problems. For example, emotions can cause an otherwise rational person to act in ways that are clearly contrary to his best interests, such as yelling at an officer who is doing little more than attempting to keep the peace or to issue a traffic citation. What is it about emotion that causes people to behave in ways that are so clearly irrational? More important, what can we do to communicate effectively with irate, frustrated, and difficult people?

THE EMOTIONAL BRAIN

Over the past few decades, neuroscientists have learned a great deal about the origins and roles of emotions. This includes the identification and study of specific brain regions responsible for both logic and emotion. As human beings we are, by our very nature, emotional. Whether we realize it or not, emotions touch every aspect of our lives. Emotions influence not only how we make choices but also what we think about. While Descartes's notion of a disembodied mind is almost certainly wrong, it appears that he may have been right about one thing: We are literally of two minds—one emotional, the other logical. The emotional brain is intuitive, fast, and instinctual. It is concerned primarily with emotional significance and with survival. The logical brain, in contrast, is rational, slow, and heavily influenced by experience. It is concerned with precision, logic, and getting things right. Together the two brains integrate thinking and feeling in ways that make the many nuances and complexities of our intellectual and emotional lives possible (see Table 2.1).

Table 2.1 Emotional Brain Versus Logical Brain

Emotional Brain	Logical Brain
Automatic	Controlled
Fast	Slow
Intuitive	Rational
Effortless	Effortful
Learns slowly	Learns quickly
Requires little energy	Requires considerable energy

SOURCE: Adapted from Lehrer, J. (2009). *How we decide.* New York: Mariner Books.

We don't normally think of our brains as collections of distinct parts, each responsible for particular functions, such as basic life support, vision, speech, logic, movement, memory, and emotion. Rather, we experience our brains as fully integrated units, capable of combining logic and emotion into one seamless experience. Scientists, however, divide the brain into three major areas: the brain stem, the limbic system, and the cerebral cortex (see Table 2.2). This division, although somewhat artificial, can nonetheless help to clarify the basic structures responsible for different functions and assist us in better understanding the relationship between logic and emotion.

Brain Stem Functions

The brain stem, or reptilian brain, as it is sometimes labeled, is a continuation of the spinal cord. It is responsible for basic vegetative functions, including the regulation of heart rate, breathing, sleeping, eating, and consciousness. The brain stem also connects the sensory nerves and motor nerves of the brain to the rest of the body. All information relayed from the brain to the body and vice versa travels through the brain stem. Damage to the brain stem can result in coma or death.

Limbic System Functions

The limbic system, or emotional brain, comprises the clusters of nuclei associated with emotions, particularly fear. It is not truly a separate system; rather, it is a collection of structures that include the hippocampus,

Table 2.2 Brain Functions

Brain Stem	Limbic System	Cerebral Cortex
Regulation of cardiac and respiratory functions	Emotional arousal	Thinking
	Fear	Planning
Consciousness	Learning	Logic
Regulation of the sleep cycle	Memory	Memory
Eating	Motivation	Language

SOURCE: Adapted from Carter, R. (1999). *Mapping the mind.* Berkeley: University of California Press.

amygdalae, anterior thalamic nuclei, septum, limbic cortex, and fornix. In addition to emotional arousal, the limbic system plays important roles in motivation, learning, and memory.

Cerebral Cortex Functions

The cerebral cortex, or logical brain, is the region commonly referred to as gray matter. The cerebral cortex is divided into right and left hemispheres. It encompasses approximately two-thirds of the brain's mass and lies over and around most of the brain's other structures. It is the most recently evolved part of the human brain and is responsible for thinking, logic, planning, learning, memory, and language.

One especially important part of the logical brain is the prefrontal cortex, the region located just behind the forehead. It is the brain area responsible for impulse control as well as learning about the social norms and values of a person's culture. The frontal cortex is the last part of the brain to develop, typically maturing around age 25—a fact that explains much of the impulsive behavior common among young adults. Although all mammals possess some functioning frontal cortex, the area is most highly developed in human beings.

Understanding the various brain structures and their functions is an important step in recognizing how and why people become emotionally distressed, as well as why it can be so difficult to reason with a person who is distraught. Losing control, failing to respond to reason, and, in some cases, behaving violently can all be traced to specific areas of the brain.

LOGIC VERSUS EMOTION

Our thoughts, decisions, and actions are the products of the two brains: one rational, the other emotional. The rational brain thinks. It performs detailed analyses of data from the outside world, compares that information to past events stored in long-term memory, and plans the best course of action. The rational brain is responsible for conscious thought, logic, planning, and language. It is also tasked with using the information gathered by our senses to create a cohesive picture of the world. The neocortex, which represents the crowning achievement of millions of years of evolutionary pressure, is primarily responsible for the rise and dominance of human beings over other species.

In contrast to the cold, logical analysis of the more recently evolved neocortex, the emotional brain feels. It is responsible for emotions like anger, fear, and love. It is also the source of our intuitions, or "gut feelings." One particularly important cluster of neurons is the amygdala, a set of structures located deep beneath the brain's temporal lobe. The amygdala specializes in emotions, especially those associated with fear. It continuously scans the environment for potential threats and activates the body's alarm, commonly referred to as the "fight or flight" response, at the first sign of danger. Unlike the slower, more logical neocortex, the emotional brain is designed for speed rather than accuracy.

Normally the two brains operate as a tightly orchestrated system. We are able to connect feeling with thinking and thinking with feeling in ways that allow us to integrate our two ways of knowing. There is a comfortable balance. On one hand, we use feelings to inform our rational brain, to help us make decisions, and to add color to logic. On the other hand, we integrate information from our rational brain to better inform feelings and occasionally to override unhealthy emotional responses. In most instances, our thoughts and feelings work together as one coordinated unit, but this is not always the case. There are times when the emotional brain seizes control, filling us with rage, anger, or other strong emotions, and leaving us seemingly beyond the reach of logic or reason.

"FIGHT OR FLIGHT"

The human brain developed from the bottom up. Because the higher brain centers of the neocortex developed as elaborations from the more primitive emotional brain, the two brains are connected by a network of neurons that allow us to integrate thoughts and feelings. We are able to "think" about our "feelings" as well as to articulate our emotions and intuitions. These connections also provide the more primitive emotional brain with a way of overriding the neocortex during an emergency— even if temporarily—to ensure our survival.

Anytime the emotional brain senses a threat (real or perceived), it activates the sympathetic branch of the autonomic nervous system, triggering the release of adrenaline and glucocorticoids into the bloodstream to prime the mind and body for action (see Table 2.3). This produces a rush of nervous energy and muscular tension, which we experience as an elevated heart rate, rapid breathing, dry mouth, sweaty palms, and butterflies in the stomach. We may also find ourselves behaving in uncharacteristically aggressive ways, such as pointing our fingers, clenching our fists, or yelling. Not surprisingly, strong emotions can make it especially difficult for us to listen or to concentrate. The more intense the feeling, the more dominant the emotional brain.

The body's stress response has been etched into the human nervous system over hundreds of millennia and thousands of generations.

Table 2.3   Stress Response (Fight or Flight)

Activation of the sympathetic branch of the autonomic nervous system ("hot" go system)
Release of glucocorticoids, including adrenaline, noradrenaline, and cortisol
Increases in heart rate and respiration
Elevation in blood pressure
Flushing or paling
Inhibition of stomach/digestive functions
Dilation of pupils
Constriction of blood vessels
Diversion of blood to large muscle groups
Tunnel vision
Shaking/tremors
Inhibition of tear production and salivation
Increase in blood sugar
Suppression of immune system
Increase in blood clotting

SOURCE: Adapted from Kagan, J. (1998). *Galen's prophecy: Temperament in human nature*. Boulder, CO: Basic Books.

As hunter-gatherers, our ancestors faced an untold number of dangers, including hungry predators, aggressive neighboring tribes, and unpredictable turns of nature. When our ancestors encountered hungry predators, they did not have the time to pause and formulate the most logical response. They needed a system capable of almost instantaneous action. The emotional brain, with its ability to prime the mind and body for an immediate response, provided the advantage necessary to ensure our ancestors' survival in such hostile environments. However, the rapid, emotional response that served our ancestors so well is poorly adapted to the challenges we face in modern society.

Today, our chances of encountering man-eating carnivores are virtually nonexistent. The human brain, in spite of its complexity and flexibility, has been unable to keep pace with our rapidly changing world. Over the span of a few thousand years, human life, particularly in highly developed countries, has changed so dramatically that many of our ancestors would be unable to cope.

Because our brains have failed to evolve at the same speed as the rest of our world, we continue to demonstrate the same hardwired responses to threats as our early ancestors, engaging in either "fight" or "flight." This is further complicated by the fact that the emotional brain responds to psychological threats in the same way it responds to physical threats—that is, as if our personal safety were in jeopardy. Thus, we respond to threats to our self-esteem in the same ways we respond to threats to our physical safety.

When a person is irate, frustrated, or angry, we can be almost certain that his emotional brain is running the show. The rational brain is on hold while the person focuses his energy, attention, and resources on the threat. His body is full of adrenaline. His mind is focused on the threat. And he is driven by a primitive urge to attack or to defend. His thoughts and emotions are no longer integrated. Rather than thinking rationally about the long-term consequences of his actions, he is concerned only with immediate survival.

As law enforcement professionals, how can we best respond to someone whose rational brain is disengaged? How do we motivate or persuade someone who is driven by pure emotion? Fortunately, the person's temporary insanity is just that—temporary. By correctly identifying a person's emotional state and by reconnecting with the rational brain, we can overcome many strong emotional responses, direct the person back to a state of calm, and manage conflict effectively.

A Silver Lining

The networks that link the two brains allow strong emotions to override logic during an emergency. This, however, does not mean that the rational brain has stopped working altogether. While the emotional brain prepares the mind and body for danger, the rational brain continues to analyze possible courses of action and ultimately decides on the best one. In other words, while we may have little control over our initial reaction, we can consciously affect the duration and intensity of our response. If, for example, a felony suspect reaches into his pocket, our emotional brain sounds the alarm and activates the body's stress response. Meanwhile, our rational brain continues to analyze, taking in additional details, comparing those facts to information stored in long-term memory, and continuously updating the emotional brain. When the rational brain determines that the suspect is retrieving a cell phone and not a firearm, it sends signals to turn off the alarm.

This is possible because the neural networks that connect the two brains travel in both directions (see Figure 2.1). In other words, neurons transmit messages from the emotional brain to the neocortex, and other

Figure 2.1   Connections Between the Emotional Brain and the Logical Brain

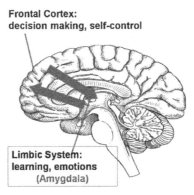

SOURCE: Adapted from Goleman, D. (1995). *Emotional intelligence: Why it can matter more than IQ*. New York: Bantam Books.

connections send signals from the neocortex to the emotional brain. These networks allow the logical brain to manage the duration and intensity of our emotional responses. Under certain conditions, however, it is possible for the rational brain not only to modify the duration and intensity of our emotions but also to override them altogether.

The connections between the rational and emotional brains offer a ray of hope, or silver lining, for managing the responses of irate, frustrated, and difficult people by providing a way of reengaging the rational brain. To manage such a person's responses effectively, we must be able to identify that individual's emotional state as well as to reengage the rational brain. This includes learning to recognize the symptoms of general arousal and other nonverbal signs of affect, including facial expressions, paralanguage, posture, proxemics, and eye contact (all of which will be discussed in greater detail later in the book). If we expect to communicate and to connect successfully, we must increase our sensitivity to the nonverbal messages of other people as well as to the messages that we send to others. This is especially true when we are dealing with irate, frustrated, and difficult people. In the same way that we watch the behaviors of others, they observe our actions as well. Transmitting the wrong messages (for example, disinterest or impatience) is almost certain to make a bad situation worse. Rather, we must make every effort to communicate interest and objectivity while using appropriate strategies to reengage the person's rational brain.

TOOLS FOR MANAGING EMOTIONS

Strong negative affective responses occur when the more primitive emotional brain triggers the body's stress response (fight or flight). When this happens, we respond emotionally rather than logically. We are less concerned with the long-term consequences of our actions than with focusing our energy and attention on the immediate threat. All of us have, at one time or another, been fearful, angry, depressed, irritated, and hostile. Emotions are entangled in every thought we have, every decision we make, and every action we take. When dealing with irate and emotional people, there is no "one size fits all" solution—no magic bullet or special phrase that will work on every person and in every instance.

The approach we should take depends on the unique environmental and personal variables of the situation as well as the number of tools we have available. The more techniques we have at our disposal, the greater our chances of success.

Be Aware of Your Response

Managing the emotions of others begins with managing our own response. Responding emotionally to someone who is already irate, frustrated, or angry will almost certainly make a bad situation worse. Everything that we do and say is potentially important. To make the right impression, we must send the right message. This means controlling our verbal and nonverbal behaviors to ensure that we communicate appropriate levels of professionalism, interest, and objectivity. Carefully monitoring our actions also allows us to influence the behavior of others by demonstrating the kinds of conduct that we want the others to model. If we appear anxious, nervous, or emotional, they will respond in kind. On the other hand, if we appear calm, professional, and interested, they are more likely to respond in ways that facilitate, rather than inhibit, successful communication and problem solving.

Listen Actively

The simple act of listening can go a long way toward reducing emotional distress. Listening provides people with important opportunities to express their feelings, attitudes, and concerns. Listening, however, is not as easy as it might appear. To listen effectively, we must do more than simply process information. Good listeners pay attention not only to people's choice of words but also to their paralanguage and other nonverbal cues. This means that we must listen with our eyes as well as with our ears. It also requires that we take an interest in others. We must learn to listen to people with the same concern and respect that we expect from others, regardless of our personal feelings.

Paraphrase

Paraphrasing involves the restatement of a person's message in another form. It can be used to clarify, summarize, or expand on the original message. Paraphrasing also offers a number of advantages for managing highly emotional people. To begin with, it allows us to interrupt someone without making things worse. For example, after listening long enough to grasp the crux of a person's complaint, an officer can politely interrupt by stating "I want to be sure that I understanding what you have told me so far" or "Okay, if I understand you correctly . . ." One of the reasons that paraphrasing is so effective is that it requires the other party to stop talking and listen to discover if the officer has, in fact, gotten the story right. Further, similar to active listening, paraphrasing provides a way of modeling appropriate behaviors and reducing tension.

Ask Questions

Strong emotions are products of the emotional brain. One way of reengaging the rational brain is to ask questions. Because answering questions requires the person to process the request, search for information, and formulate a response, questions naturally engage the rational brain. This is especially true of open-ended questions that require an extended search for information and a narrative response, such as "Tell me more about that" or "What happened next?" Unlike binary questions, narrative questions cannot be answered with a simple yes or no. The more we can engage the person in answering narrative questions, the greater our chances of reengaging the rational brain.

Let the Person Vent

One of the most effective ways of dealing with someone who is angry or frustrated is to allow the person to blow off steam. Rather than arguing, debating, or disagreeing, our best course of action is to let the person vent. The simple act of venting provides people with a form of psychological release. Our job is not to react to emotional outbursts or to personal attacks. Rather, we should listen quietly, acknowledge the person's concerns, and demonstrate interest. This includes allowing the person to have the last word. If she stops talking, we should prompt her to continue. Not only does letting someone vent allow that person to blow off steam, but it also demonstrates our patience, empathy, and genuine desire to listen.

Reframe the Problem

One final tool for managing anger, frustration, and other strong emotions is reframing. The way we frame a problem has a lot to do with how we respond. When we reframe a problem, we describe it from a different perspective while eliminating emotionally charged language. This also allows us to correct any inaccuracies in perception. For example, "What an idiot!" an irate motorist might exclaim. "I can't believe the way he cut me off!" The officer might reframe the statement this way: "If I understand correctly, you were approaching the intersection when the other driver moved into your lane, hitting the front of your car." While the problem remains unchanged, reframing the issue allows us to eliminate strong emotional language. Similar to paraphrasing and other forms of listening, reframing also allows us to demonstrate the kinds of verbal and nonverbal responses that can best facilitate a constructive dialogue.

SUMMARY

Emotions are a fact of life. When handled properly they can enhance our motivation and protect us from danger. When handled improperly, however, they can destroy careers and damage relationships. Every decision we make and every action we take is somehow influenced by emotions. To deal effectively with people, we must deal effectively with their emotions. Emotions and logic are governed by the two different brains: one logical, the other emotional. Understanding the brain regions responsible for strong emotions is an important step toward better managing irate and frustrated people. The strong urge to act when we are emotionally aroused produces a number of physiological, behavioral, and cognitive changes, which we communicate through facial expressions, posture, proxemics, eye contact, and paralanguage. Fortunately, a number of tools are available to help us better manage the emotions of others, including monitoring our response, asking questions, allowing the person to vent, paraphrasing, active listening, and reframing the problem.

Because we are dealing with humans, we need to remain flexible, open-minded, and patient. We must be flexible enough to adapt to changing circumstances and to modify our strategies when they are not working, as well as open-minded enough to continue learning and refining new techniques. We must also remain patient. Managing another person's emotions is, at best, difficult. Considerable time and patience are often required to reengage the rational brain and to reestablish meaningful communication. In the end, however, such efforts will undoubtedly make us safer and more effective.

The next chapter discusses the second step in the IMPACT model: Master the story.

STUDY QUESTIONS

1. What are the three components of emotions?
2. What are the functions of the logical brain and the emotional brain?
3. What is the purpose of the "fight or flight" response?
4. How does the "fight or flight" response interfere with a person's ability to think logically?
5. In what way do the connections between the logical brain and the emotional brain enable us to manage the responses of irate, frustrated, and difficult people?
6. List five strategies for reengaging the rational brain.

MASTER THE STORY

————•◦•————

*Most of the successful people I've known are the ones who do more
listening than talking.*

—Bernard M. Baruch

Courses in communication often emphasize the importance of speaking and presentation skills while downplaying the importance of listening. This overlooks the simple fact that we spend more time listening than we do in any other type of communication activity. Studies have shown listening to be the single most important skill for entry-level workers, supervisors, and managers, influencing career success, productivity, and organizational effectiveness. Good listening skills are also a vital part of dealing effectively with people who are irate, frustrated, or emotional. This is because the better we understand a problem, the more successful we are at diagnosing issues, establishing rapport, promoting positive behavior, managing conflict, and soothing negative emotions. However, despite the importance of listening, law enforcement agencies provide surprisingly little training in this area.

While most of us acknowledge that listening is important, actually becoming a good listener can be remarkably difficult. Listening well is a demanding and complex process. To begin with, listening is a skill much like speaking. We all listen, but few of us do it well. There is also a difference between hearing and listening. Hearing is a physiological process that takes place when sound waves strike the eardrum at a particular frequency, causing vibrations that are transmitted to the brain. In contrast, listening is the process of making sense of another person's message. Good listening requires patience, energy, and genuine concern for the other person.

We often think of hearing and listening as the same activity. We believe that if we have heard another person's message, we have listened. We seldom stop to think about what it means to listen or how we can be more effective listeners. Listening does not occur automatically. When we confuse hearing with listening, we mislead ourselves into believing that we really understand others when we are only hearing sounds. Because we spend a great deal of time interacting with others, we often assume that we are good listeners. Unfortunately, studies have found that there is no relationship between how competently we think we listen and how well we actually understand others. The good news is that with the right combination of attitude and practice, we can all improve our listening skills.

MINDLESS LISTENING VERSUS MINDFUL LISTENING

Listening is hard work, even for the most enthusiastic communicators. We hear all the time without truly listening. Sometimes we deliberately ignore sounds and people. Indeed, most of us find it easy to block out annoying noises, such as television commercials and unrelated conversations. Other times, we are so overwhelmed by information and demands on our attention that we simply cannot help but miss important messages. While there may be times when ignoring others is necessary, we should recognize that doing so can cause us to miss valuable information. It can also damage our abilities to communicate and to connect with others by limiting our understanding of their problems.

In addition to the difference between hearing and listening, we do not process all messages in the same way. Listening can be divided into two basic types: mindless and mindful. When we engage in mindless listening, we react to the messages of others automatically, without any real mental effort. While it may seem counterproductive for us to stroll mindlessly through our daily lives, some degree of mindlessness is a necessary evil. This is because the amount of information that we can process is limited. Indeed, many experts on cognition argue that we are incapable of processing fully more than one piece of information at a time. By being selective about which messages we ignore and which we process, we save our mental energy for only the most important people and ideas.

The second type of listening, mindful listening, involves the careful and thoughtful analysis of others' messages. We are more likely to listen mindfully when a message is personally important or when it is delivered by someone we care about or respect. Mindful listening requires our full attention and energy. It entails not only listening to the other person's words but also observing the person's body language and tone of voice and being alert for signs of anger, frustration, and other emotions. Our tendency to listen mindlessly is one of the main reasons that relationships fail, problems remain unresolved, and conflicts spiral out of control.

BARRIERS TO EFFECTIVE LISTENING

Even careful listening does not guarantee that we will send and receive messages accurately. Every attempt to communicate with others is complicated by some form of "noise"—that is, anything that disrupts or distorts the message's intended meaning. Noise can be divided into two types: physiological and psychological. Physiological noise comes from biological factors that make it difficult to communicate accurately, such as illness, fatigue, or hearing loss. At the end of a long shift, for example, an officer can find it difficult to listen mindfully because of fatigue or hunger.

Psychological noise, on the other hand, results from internal forces that interfere with the sending or receiving of messages. Anytime two or more people listen to the same information, we typically assume that they have received and understood the same message, but this is simply not the case. Because everyone brings a different set of expectations, beliefs, values, assumptions, and goals to the process, no two people, regardless of how similar they are in background and experience, will interpret the same message in exactly the same way.

The ways that we make sense of and respond to the messages of others are affected by a combination of physiological and psychological factors. In most cases, however, the greatest barriers to mindful listening are not physiological (noise or hearing loss, for example) but psychological (expectations or closed-mindedness, for example). In fact, nothing can derail our efforts to build rapport and gather information faster than the pre-existing ideas, assumptions, and stereotypes held by the people involved. While a certain amount of mindless listening is inevitable, we need to be aware of the many obstacles to good listening so that we can avoid them during those times when listening really counts.

Past Experiences and Expectations

Our past experiences shape what we expect to see and hear. It is a fact that we don't see the world as it is; rather, we see what we expect to see. Anytime we look hard enough for something, there is a good chance that we will find it. A person who was treated rudely by an officer in the past may expect to be treated in a similar way every time she encounters law enforcement in the future. Not surprisingly, some-one with prior negative law enforcement experiences is more likely to judge officers as rude or hostile than someone whose prior contacts have been positive. In fact, not only is such a person likely to look selectively for evidence to confirm her beliefs, she is also more likely to overlook positive behaviors that don't fit her expectations.

Stereotypes and Prejudices

Stereotypes and prejudices are types of hasty generalizations based on limited evidence. While we are all prone to snap judgments, stereo-types and prejudices can be especially damaging. They can cause us to pay attention to only those aspects of a person or message that confirm the stereotype or prejudice, while ignoring others. This often occurs when we encounter people whose ideas or interests are different from our own. The same is true of criticism. We are less likely to listen to and consider criticism from those we have stereotyped negatively, despite the fact that their comments may be true.

Closed-mindedness

Closed-mindedness can occur anytime we believe that we have noth-ing new to learn about a person or topic. When we close our minds to the ideas, information, and feelings of others, we limit our understanding of those persons and their problems, as well as our ability to offer solutions. In order to solve problems, resolve conflicts, and deal effectively with irate, frustrated, and difficult people, we must remain flexible and open-minded, regardless of our personal opinions, feelings, and past experiences.

Faulty Assumptions

We all make assumptions. Sometimes our assumptions are right; other times, they are wrong. When our assumptions are right, they serve us well. However, when they are wrong, they can damage our abilities to listen and to communicate effectively. Whenever we assume that we know more than we really do, we are likely to stop listening. The same thing happens when we erroneously assume that a problem is so simple or so transparent that the answer is self-evident. Mindful listening requires us to be aware of our assumptions. It also requires us to take precautions to ensure that our assumptions don't interfere with our abilities to gather information and to connect with others.

Preoccupation

Anytime we are preoccupied with our own thoughts, feelings, and needs (for example, we might be thinking about how we are going to find the time to handle our pending calls for service as well as to complete our remaining reports before the end of watch), we find it difficult to give others our full attention. While it is only natural to place one's own needs above those of others, we must be aware that mindful listening is possible only when we offer the other person our full attention. This requires that we suspend, at least temporarily, our own concerns.

Information Overload

We are simply incapable of processing all of the messages that we are exposed to every day. Even under the most ideal conditions, we can find it nearly impossible to focus on every detail of other people's messages, much less when we are preoccupied, closed-minded, or fatigued.

We should be aware that when this happens, we might choose, either consciously or unconsciously, to listen mindlessly rather than mindfully to others.

Effort

Mindful listening is difficult under the best of conditions. It can quickly drain our limited resources of physical and mental energy. In many cases, it doesn't take long for the effects of listening carefully to show. Once fatigue sets in, we become less willing to listen mindfully, less tolerant of others, and less likely to put forth the effort necessary to understand others and their problems.

Rapid Cognition

The final barrier to effective listening, rapid cognition, is physiological in nature. The human brain is an amazing machine. We have the capacity to process information more rapidly than others can speak. Our brains can understand as many as 600 words per minute, while the average person speaks between 100 and 150 words per minute. We often use this space (the space between 100 and 600 words a minute) to daydream, to plan our responses, or to ignore the other person altogether. This can cause us to overlook or to misinterpret important words and behaviors, hindering our abilities to connect with others, manage strong emotions, and solve problems.

DEVELOPING THE RIGHT ATTITUDE

Listening effectively is as much about attitude as it is about skill. We often assume that we know more about a person or a situation than we really do. This can limit our curiosity and lessen our willingness to learn. Instead of staying curious, we jump to conclusions. Rather than remaining flexible, we make assumptions. In place of learning, we close our minds. Mindful listening begins with an attitude of heartfelt curiosity. This means that rather than simply going through the motions, we try honestly to understand the situation from the other person's perspective. Instead of reacting reflexively or plotting our next response, we do everything possible to engage the person in meaningful dialogue by asking questions, listening to his answers, and taking a genuine interest in the person and his problem.

When we listen mindfully to others, we do so because we want to gain a better understanding of their thoughts, feelings, and behaviors. To understand a person or problem fully, we must engage the other party in meaningful dialogue. One of the best ways to facilitate dialogue is to ask open-ended questions. Unlike closed-ended questions, which require nothing more than yes or no responses, open-ended questions do not limit a person's replies. For example, questions such as "What happened?" or "Can you tell me what's going on?" cannot be answered with a simple yes or no. Rather, they require narrative responses. Open-ended questions allow people to build their answers around what they believe are the most important issues. The information provided then sets the stage for follow-up questions, which should reflect the same formula. Examples of follow-up questions include "What happened next?" and "Can you give me an example?" Open-ended initial questions and follow-up questions are both important, and both can generate valuable information.

Asking the right questions is important; however, doing so is of little value unless we approach the conversation with the right attitude. This is not a trivial point. Our words and behaviors reflect our attitude. Our attitude—as well as the words and behaviors that follow—should communicate interest in the person and her problem. Displaying such an attitude is not always easy, especially when we are dealing with someone who resists or refuses to cooperate. While it may be natural to react to resistance by pressing our point, this approach is usually not very effective. The harder we push, the harder the other person resists. Contrary to popular belief, the best way to overcome resistance is to apply less pressure, not more. If we want others to hear what we have to say, we must first listen to what they have to say. If we want others to acknowledge our concerns, we must first acknowledge their concerns. If we want to persuade others, we need to listen, not talk. Indeed, listening with an attitude of sincerity, curiosity, and patience is arguably the single most important tool that we have for motivating and persuading others.

Sincerity

If we expect others to engage us in meaningful dialogue, we must be sincere. The way a person sees us, our interests, and our reasons for asking will affect his decision to tell his story and how much of it he is willing to share. Simply put, perception matters. Before we can convince another person to share his thoughts and feelings, we must first communicate genuine interest in the person and his problem. Others can usually see through disingenuous attempts to appear sincere and often react to such attempted deception with anger. People pay attention not only to our words but also to our nonverbal messages, including our posture, facial expressions, and eye contact. If our body language and emotions are insincere, nothing else that we do (for example, how intently we appear to listen or how sincerely we attempt to behave) will really matter.

Curiosity

In order to establish and maintain a dialogue, we must create an environment in which the person feels safe to talk. This includes demonstrating appropriate levels of curiosity and open-mindedness. Genuine curiosity permits us to withhold judgment until we fully understand the facts. Rather than jumping to conclusions, we remain open to new information and ideas. Open-mindedness allows us to acknowledge that there is always something more to learn about the person and about his problem. Simply put, the longer we withhold judgment and the more we know, the better our abilities to diagnose the problem and to find workable solutions.

Patience

Understanding and listening can be hard work. Considerable time, patience, and persistence are often required to gather enough information to fully understand a person's thoughts and feelings. To complicate matters, people are usually reluctant to share their thoughts and feelings with someone they do not know very well. This is especially true when people are irritated, frustrated, or emotional. Adrenaline and other bodily chemicals that fuel strong emotions often require considerable time to dissipate. During that time, a person's thoughts, feelings, and behaviors can vary considerably. What was important one moment can be completely forgotten in the next. People often need time to figure out why they are upset or emotional. This means that if we hope to get to the root cause of a problem, we need to be especially patient.

EIGHT-STEP STRATEGY FOR EFFECTIVE LISTENING

While mindful listening may appear to be a single process, it actually consists of several activities that occur simultaneously or in rapid succession. We can improve our abilities to listen and to respond by breaking up the listening process into the following eight specific, easily managed behaviors.

Step 1: Offer an Invitation

The first step to engaging someone in meaningful dialogue—that is, a respectful exchange of information and ideas—is to offer an invitation. Friends do not intimidate or coerce one another into providing information. People choose whether or not to participate in a dialogue because they have something to say or because they want to hear what the other person has to offer. In other words, both parties must decide whether or not to participate and, if they participate, how much information they are willing to share. One way of improving our odds that a person will participate is to offer an invitation. We might say, for example, "Sir, I would like your help in better understanding what's going on," or ask, "Ma'am, do you mind talking about what happened?"

Step 2: Eliminate Distractions

Distractions come in two forms: external and internal. External distractions are the things occurring around us—for example, ringing telephones, traffic, and radio communications. Internal distractions are the physiological and psychological influences that interfere with our abilities to listen and to communicate effectively. Before we attempt to facilitate a meaningful dialogue, we should eliminate all possible distractions. This might include, among other things, turning off the telephone, turning down the radio or television, and closing the office door.

Step 3: Pay Attention

The third step is to devote our full attention and energy to the other person. Mindful listening requires us to do more than simply listen to a person's words. We must listen with both our ears and our eyes. In other words, we should listen not only to the person's words but also to her voice (for example, pitch, tone, and cadence) and observe her nonverbal behaviors (for example, facial expressions, gaze, and posture). Because the messages that people send are communicated through a combination of verbal and nonverbal signals, we need to pay close attention to the interplay of both types of messages to maximize our listening effectiveness.

Step 4: Listen for Key Words

When people speak, they often provide important insights into their thoughts, feelings, and concerns. Most of the time, neither the speaker nor the listener picks up on these clues. This makes it especially important for us to listen actively to the person's words and behaviors, including listening for background messages, key words, and unspoken emotions, many of which are communicated nonverbally. Identifying key words and emotions can be especially helpful as we try to define issues, formulate questions, and guide the conversation.

Step 5: Acknowledge

When someone fails to listen, we often assume that it is because the person doesn't care. This is almost never the case. The main reason that others fail to listen is because they don't feel heard. Before we can expect a person to listen to our concerns, we must first acknowledge his concerns. Acknowledging a person is one of the simplest and most cost-effective ways of demonstrating empathy, interest, and sincerity, all of which are critical to effective listening.

Step 6: Provide Feedback

One of the best ways to demonstrate interest and involvement while listening is to provide appropriate feedback, which can be verbal or nonverbal. Verbal feedback involves prompts such as "Okay" or "Please go on," as well as requests for clarification or more information, such as "Please tell me more about that" or "Can you give me an example of what you mean?" Nonverbal feedback can take such forms as head nodding, making eye contact, and offering appropriate facial expressions. Both types are important, and we should use both types anytime we interact with others.

Step 7: Mirror Feelings

When we mirror another's feelings, we describe what we are seeing and hearing from the other person. Mirroring can be especially helpful when a person's words and behaviors don't match. A person may say, for example, that she "feels fine" while her voice and body tell a different story: her face is fixed in a scowl, her posture is closed, and she refuses to make eye contact. Mirroring provides a way of describing how the person's words are saying one thing while her voice and body are sending a different message. This not only provides the person with important feedback but also gives her the opportunity to revisit or to clarify her thoughts and feelings.

Step 8: Paraphrase and Clarify

Paraphrasing involves restating the person's problem and concerns in our own words. This allows the person to hear his words and problem framed in a slightly different way. It also allows us to check for accuracy and understanding. If our understanding of the problem is wrong, the person can provide us with immediate feedback. We should never try to diagnose or solve a person's problem without first checking with the person for understanding. Simply put, if we don't understand the problem, we are in no position to offer solutions.

WHAT TO AVOID

In contrast to the behaviors described above, which can help us better understand others and their problems, certain behaviors seldom, if ever, improve the quality of our interaction with others. These should be avoided, as they usually do little more than make a bad situation worse.

Premature Judgments

It can be difficult, if not impossible, to understand a person's behaviors and feelings fully without passing judgment. As we have already seen, everyone is prone to snap judgments and first impressions. However, we need to be careful about how those judgments influence our attitudes and behaviors. When we form a positive first impression of someone, we are more likely to remain open and interested in the person's thoughts and feelings. On the other hand, when we form a negative first impression, we are less apt to invest the time and energy necessary to better understand the person or her problem. Although we cannot eliminate snap judgments altogether, we can raise our level of awareness. If we find ourselves judging others too harshly or too soon, we can make a deliberate effort to remain neutral and to listen actively until we more fully understand the problem.

Planning Responses

It can be difficult to maintain the mental energy and focus necessary to listen to someone talk about his problems and feelings for an extended period of time, even under the best of circumstances. Rather than listening mindfully, we often find that our attention has drifted. Before we know it, we are too lost in our own thoughts or too busy thinking about our next responses to actually listen to the person's message. To listen effectively, to connect with others, and to understand their problems fully, we must suspend our thoughts and concerns while offering nothing less than our undivided attention.

Wolves in Sheep's Clothing

Good questions are arguably the single most powerful tools that we have for gaining information, diagnosing problems, and soothing strong emotions. Good questions provide a way of learning more about people and their problems. Thus, we should use questions as learning tools, not as value judgments. This means that we should never disguise assertions or judgments as questions. Doing so only confuses people. It also creates resentment and resistance. For example, "Why did you start arguing with him?" and "Did you have to call her names?" are accusations, not questions. Judgments and assertions disguised as questions do nothing to provide us with the kind of information we need to understand people and their problems. Rather than help us engage others in meaningful dialogue, questions like these usually do little more than put people on the defensive, stifle further communication, and inhibit collective problem solving.

Cross-Examination

While the purpose of questions is to gather information, the object of cross-examination is to point out flaws in a person's argument. For example, "If you tried everything that you could to avoid fighting with her, why did you yell at her?" and "I guess you think that I am responsible for this, but how many mistakes did you make?" are nothing more than thinly veiled attempts to prove the other person wrong. People typically respond to cross-examination with irritation and defensiveness. Rather than facilitating meaningful dialogue, cross-examination makes it more difficult to diagnose problems and to find solutions. Before we ask a question, we should first examine our motives for doing so. If our goal is to better understand the person or the problem, we should go ahead and ask. On the other hand, if our goal is to prove that we are smarter than the other person or to prove that we are right, we need to revisit our reasons or rethink our questions.

Closed-Ended Questions

Closed-ended questions force a person to choose between limited possible responses, often yes or no—for example, "Did you start the argument?" or "Did you swerve into the other lane of traffic?" In many cases, closed-ended questions imply that there is only one right answer. Such questions naturally limit the amount of information that we receive. We should keep in mind that the longer a person speaks, the better our chances of gaining information, and the more we are able to learn. Whenever possible, we should avoid using closed-ended questions, opting instead for open-ended inquiries that require narrative responses. This improves our chances of engaging the person in meaningful dialogue and enhances the quality of information that we receive.

SUMMARY

Mindful listening is hard work. Every attempt we make to communicate with others is complicated by some form of noise, either physiological or psychological. In most cases, the greatest barriers to mindful listening are not physiological but psychological. These include past experiences and expectations, stereotypes and prejudices, closed-mindedness, faulty assumptions, preoccupation, information overload, and rapid cognition. To complicate matters further, we often assume that we know more about a person or problem than we really do. Assuming that we have nothing new to learn dampens our curiosity, limits our flexibility, and undermines our willingness to listen. Contrary to popular belief, the best way to influence others is not to talk but to listen.

Mindful listening begins with an attitude of genuine curiosity. We listen to others because we care about what they have to say—that is, because we believe that their thoughts and feelings have value. In other words, we listen because we believe that what they have to offer will help us better understand the problem and identify possible solutions. Mindful listening is not a single activity; rather, it involves several processes occurring simultaneously or in rapid succession. The steps to effective listening include offering an invitation, eliminating distractions, paying attention, listening for key words, acknowledging, providing feedback, mirroring, and paraphrasing. The good news is that with the right combination of attitude and practice, we can all improve our abilities to listen and to gather information.

The next chapter outlines the third step in the IMPACT model: Promote positive behavior.

STUDY QUESTIONS

1. What are the differences between mindless listening and mindful listening?

2. Describe the differences between physiological noise and psychological noise.

3. List three obstacles to mindful listening.

4. Why is the right attitude important for mindful listening?

5. Explain the eight steps for effective listening.

6. List three obstacles we should avoid when trying to gain a better understanding of others.

⊰ 4 ⊱

PROMOTE POSITIVE BEHAVIOR

———•◦•———

People don't change their behavior unless it makes a difference for them to do so.

—Fran Tarkenton

Regardless of how good we are at managing emotions or listening, we won't be very effective at dealing with others unless we can gain their willing cooperation. Too often, officers believe it is their job to issue orders, and it is the job of others to follow those orders. As law enforcement professionals, we have tremendous authority, including the powers to detain, search, and arrest. Nonetheless, our abilities to compel or coerce others are limited. To begin with, most of the people we encounter are not hardened criminals but honest, hardworking citizens, just like us. They might be emotional, they might be frustrated, they might be having a bad day, or they might be experiencing all of the above. In any case, our challenge is the same: to motivate and persuade others to do what we need them to do voluntarily, not to force compliance.

Gaining cooperation is not getting others to do what we want them to do. Rather, it is getting others to want to do what we want them to do. This is not a trivial point. In the first case, we can compel certain people under certain conditions to follow orders. Telling people what to do, however, has its limits. To begin with, most people (regardless of who they are) don't like being told what to do. When people feel pushed, they tend to push back. The harder we push, the harder they push back. If they decide to cooperate, they do so begrudgingly, doing only the minimum asked of them. Second, whenever we compel people to cooperate, we run the risk of creating anger and resentment. People who are angry at law enforcement can be quick to lodge complaints. Whether or not complaints lack merit, they become a permanent part of officers' personnel records in most law enforcement agencies. Regardless of the types or outcomes, complaints can have negative impacts on officers' consideration for promotion, special assignments, and training. Angry, frustrated, and emotional people can also be dangerous people. In extreme cases, they may lash out physically, injuring officers, themselves, or others.

It stands to reason that, despite our formal authority as peace officers, our ability to force compliance is limited. While we can compel some people to cooperate under some circumstances, we clearly lack the authority to compel everyone to cooperate under every circumstance. We can, however, use a number of tactics to promote positive behavior and get others to do what we need without resorting to coercion. Throughout this book, I use the term *positive behavior* to refer to actions that are compliant and cooperative. In other words, people demonstrate positive behavior by cooperating willingly with our requests. By getting others to cooperate voluntarily, we not only make our jobs easier and reduce complaints but also improve our safety and effectiveness in virtually every aspect of our work.

CONFLICT STYLE

The first aspect of promoting positive behavior is our style of interacting with others. Our abilities to communicate and to connect effectively are critical to building trust and rapport. Saying the right words in the right way and at the right time can go a long way toward reducing tension, soothing strong emotions, and securing cooperation. However, the reverse is also true: Saying the wrong words in the wrong way and at the wrong time can make an already bad situation even worse. Two critical aspects of communicating successfully with others are our conflict style and our words and language.

Studies have identified three basic styles of conflict communication: passive, aggressive, and assertive. Each has its own set of strengths and weaknesses. Understanding all of these styles allows us to approach our communication with others in the most productive ways possible.

Passive Style of Communication

Our goal when using a passive style is to avoid saying or doing anything that might offend the other person. We express our concerns indirectly. However, in doing so, we often fail to set appropriate limits. Because our goal is to not say or do anything offensive, we go along begrudgingly, dragging our feet while looking for ways to sabotage the agreement. The problem with passive communication is that our concerns go unrecognized and unmet. Over time, our resentment grows, and we end up blaming the other person for our failure to voice our concerns. When we have finally had enough, we go on the attack. While this approach may get us some of what we want, it can permanently damage the relationship.

Aggressive Style of Communication

In contrast to the passive style, our goal when using an aggressive style of communication is to dominate the other person and to get our way. We tell others in no uncertain terms just how wrong they are while pushing them to give us what we want. If they fail to give in, we push even harder. If they continue to hold out, we punish them. What we fail to realize is that the harder we push, the harder they push back. The more we blame others, the more they blame us. Even when they do give in, they do so reluctantly. While this tactic may get us some of what we want in the short term, the more we try to dominate others, the more their resentment grows. Over time, the relationship becomes increasingly dysfunctional, until it eventually fails completely, making meaningful communication virtually impossible.

Assertive Style of Communication

The passive and aggressive styles of communication are usually not well suited for law enforcement. We cannot wait passively for others to acknowledge our concerns. We need others to follow our directions, and we need them to do so promptly and voluntarily. On the other hand, being overly aggressive usually results in little more than resentment and resistance. People push back in an attempt to retain their freedom. They may refuse to follow simple directions, or they may refuse to cooperate altogether. Fortunately, there is a third alternative. An assertive style of communication allows us to express concerns, set limits, and motivate others in respectful ways. It provides a way of managing conflict and dealing with others without ignoring our own concerns or our safety, and without permanently damaging the relationship.

Assertive messages follow a three-part formula, referred to as a "D-E-R script":

- *Describe the behavior:* The first step is to describe the facts as we perceive them. That is, we share our observations of the person's behavior as clearly and factually as possible. We do not guess at the person's motives or speculate about thoughts, feelings, or intentions. We simply describe the behavior as factually and objectively as possible. The more objectively we describe the person's behavior, the less likely we are to trigger defensiveness or resistance.

- *Express the result:* The second step is to express the effects of the person's behavior. Again, we need to explain the results as factually and objectively as possible, without overdramatizing, blaming, or mind reading. In other words, what were the outcomes of the person's behavior? For example, did the behavior result in an unnecessary delay? Did the behavior result in additional work? Did the behavior further aggravate someone who was already emotionally distressed?

- *Request what you want:* The final step is to request a specific change in behavior. We need to remember that we cannot change another person's personality, values, or beliefs. Therefore, asking someone to change her attitude is pointless. It is simply too vague. "You need to have a better attitude," we might say. "How do you know what my attitude is?" the person responds. "My attitude is fine!" Rather, we should focus on specific, objective behaviors. The more explicit we are with our request, the better our chances of getting what we want.

The following scenario, involving an officer attempting to resolve a family dispute, provides an example of assertive communication. Each time the officer presents the wife with a set of options, she interrupts by yelling, "This is his fault!" The officer then describes the wife's behavior in specific, objective terms (the first step in the D-E-R script): "Ma'am, each time I offer a solution, you interrupt me by yelling." Next, the officer outlines the result of her behavior (the second step): "By interrupting me, you make it more difficult to resolve this." Finally, the officer describes the desired change in the woman's behavior (the third step): "What I need from you is to let me finish speaking; otherwise, I cannot be of any help."

Again, it is important to note that assertive communication includes specific requests for changes in behavior, rather than vague requests to modify attitudes or beliefs. Ambiguous statements like "I need you to be more helpful" are simply too fuzzy. The more specific the request, the more likely we are to get what we need.

Words and Language

In addition to selecting our style of communication carefully, we need to be sensitive about the words and language we choose. Words are powerful. The language that we choose can aggravate an already difficult situation or help move us closer to agreement. This is especially true when we are interacting with people who are irate, frustrated, or emotional. Rather than attempt to coerce others to our way of thinking, we should strive for a balance of confidence and humility. This usually requires that we take a softer approach, such as changing our truths to perceptions and changing our conclusions to hypotheses. For example, we could soften "The fact of the matter is" to "If I understand correctly." Or we might modify "It seems clear to me that" to "It appears that." Tempering our language in this way can reduce defensiveness while making it safe for others to offer their views.

A second way we can increase our chances of communicating and connecting with others is to focus the discussion on our own thoughts and feelings rather than on their behaviors. As discussed in more depth in Chapter 7, we should avoid reading too much into others' behaviors. Referring to our own thoughts and behaviors, however, can be an effective way to facilitate a dialogue. We do this by replacing "you" statements with "I" statements (see Table 4.1). Because "you" statements express judgments about others, they often create resentment and resistance.

Table 4.1 "You" Statements Versus "I" Statements

"You" Statement	"I" Statement
You are making me angry.	I am feeling angry.
You obviously don't get it.	I am not making myself clear.
You need to listen.	I need to better explain myself.
You only care about yourself.	I need to better understand your perspective.
You are not explaining things very well.	I am not doing a good job of understanding.

SOURCE: Adapted from Adler, R. B., & Proctor, R. F., II. (2007). *Looking out/looking in* (12th ed.). Belmont, CA: Thomson Higher Education.

For example, statements such as "You are making me mad!" or "You obviously don't get it!" are likely to provoke defensive responses. Most of us do not like to admit our mistakes, even when we are clearly wrong. "I" statements, on the other hand, allow us to communicate our thoughts and concerns without accusing the other person of wrongdoing.

"I" statements allow us to reframe a problem in a way that describes the impact of the person's behavior without challenging his thoughts or feelings. Statements such as "I don't understand" and "Perhaps I could have explained myself better" are nonaccusatory and, therefore, less likely to prompt defensive responses. One reason "I" statements are effective is that we are not telling the other person what to think, what to feel, or what to do. Rather, we are simply being honest about what we are thinking and feeling.

Even the best "I" statements, however, will not be very helpful unless they are delivered in the right way. "I" statements work best when our verbal and nonverbal messages are harmonious. If our words are neutral but our voice tone, facial expression, and body language all send accusatory messages, we are likely to promote resentment and resistance. To be successful in using "I" statements, we must describe our thoughts, feelings, and opinions while avoiding the appearance of judgment. Our goal is to explain the effects of the person's behavior, not to evaluate the behavior's worth.

While "I" statements can increase our chances of being heard, nothing works in every situation. None of us wants to hear how our behavior caused problems for others, regardless of how the message is delivered.

In other cases, we are simply too entrenched or too emotionally invested to listen, regardless of the approach. Nonetheless, "I" statements will almost always improve our chances of success without making things worse.

REMOVE THE BARRIERS

Anytime we deal with irate, frustrated, or difficult people, we can expect to encounter a number of predictable barriers. In order to build rapport, gather information, and promote positive behavior, we need to recognize and remove these obstacles. Three of the most common problems are failing to meet the person's basic needs, discounting the person's involvement in the process, and disregarding the person's need to save face.

Meet the Person's Basic Needs

Despite our individual differences, all human beings share a number of basic needs. We can increase our chances of promoting positive behavior and gaining voluntary cooperation by recognizing, acknowledging, and fulfilling these needs. The following are some of our most important needs:

- Safety and security
- Status
- Self-esteem
- Recognition
- Control
- Sense of belonging
- Sense of achievement

While each of these needs is important, this list fails to include one of the most basic, yet often overlooked, human motivations: the need for respect. Our need for respect runs through virtually every aspect of our personal and professional lives. Respect encompasses esteem, status, and recognition. It also involves our needs for fundamental fairness and equality. It is important to note that treating another with respect is unrelated to how we actually feel about the person. We can have positive feelings about a person without respecting his behavior. On the other hand, we can respect someone we do not like. We can respect someone for being honest, hardworking, or talented but also have no interest in getting to know the person better. When we fail to show respect for an individual, the conversation is no longer about the original problem. It is now about defending one's self-worth. As history has demonstrated repeatedly, people will go to great lengths—including a willingness to die, in some cases—to defend their dignity and self-respect.

If we hope to establish a meaningful dialogue, we must continuously honor the other person's basic humanity, including the needs for respect, dignity, and self-esteem, regardless of our personal feelings. Part of doing so is taking the person's interests and ideas seriously. In almost every case, failing to honor a person's basic needs is a surefire recipe for disaster.

Give the Person a Stake in the Outcome

It can be one thing to reach a resolution but another thing altogether to get a person's buy-in. Too often we focus only on the outcome while ignoring the process. As discussed earlier, process matters. Others are interested not only in the outcome but also in the process that was used to arrive at the decision. One way to ensure a proper outcome is to give the other party a stake in the process—that is, involve the other person in the decision-making process. Involving the other person is more than a technical exercise. It is human nature to reject the decisions of others, regardless of how favorable the outcome, anytime we feel excluded from the process.

One way of involving the other person is to solicit advice. We might ask, for example, "How do you suggest we resolve things?" or "What advice can you offer on how to best solve this?" By asking for advice, we acknowledge the other person, her concerns, and her role in the process. This includes giving the person credit for any ideas wherever possible. A second tactic is to offer the person a choice. For instance, "It appears that we have two options, which one do you prefer?" Once the person selects an option, it becomes her idea. This increases the person's psychological and emotional investment. The simple truth of the matter is that we are always more willing to take ownership of a decision when we have invested in the process.

Allow the Person to Save Face

A third consideration when communicating with someone who is irate, frustrated, or emotional is that person's need to save face—that is, to preserve his dignity, pride, or prestige. Sometimes we want so badly to save face that we agree to do something that is clearly against our best interests. Allowing a person to save face is not the same as making excuses for his bad behavior. Rather, it is about offering the person a way to maintain his self-respect and dignity. None of us like to admit when we are wrong, especially when we can avoid it. We allow others to save face by focusing on workable solutions rather than on assigning blame.

It is important to note that our interactions with others do not occur in a vacuum. There are almost always audiences of friends, neighbors, coworkers, or family members whose opinions we value. It is only natural to want to avoid the appearance of being weak or backing down. In many cases, people will continue to hold out in a dispute simply to avoid the appearance of selling out. Our job is to frame a problem in a way that allows the person to save face while we ensure that our most important concerns are addressed.

ASK FOR A COMMITMENT

When people give their word, we expect them to follow through. That is, we expect consistency between what people tell us they are going to do and what they actually do. We often criticize people who say one thing and do something else, labeling them as liars or hypocrites, and we tend to view people whose words and behaviors are consistent as stable and honest. One way of motivating positive behavior and compliance is to secure a public commitment. This might include, for example, a person's guarantee to respect others. When people go on record with a commitment, they have a natural tendency to maintain consistency between their words and their behaviors.

When we say one thing but do another, the disconnect produces psychological and emotional discomfort, something psychologists refer to as cognitive dissonance. For example, a person who talks about the importance of treating others with respect but behaves disrespectfully can experience feelings of dissonance. The person has two options to relieve the discomfort: He can either change his behavior by treating others respectfully or rationalize his actions by creating an excuse for his behavior.

The human tendency to maintain consistency provides us with a powerful tool for promoting positive behavior and gaining cooperation. If we can secure a person's commitment to treat others respectfully, to listen while others speak, or to work collaboratively with others, we can motivate positive behavior by reminding the person of that commitment. It is worth noting, however, that this approach will work only when the person is forced to conclude that she is solely responsible for any disparity between her beliefs and her actions.

Techniques Based on Commitment and Consistency

Salespersons and other compliance professionals have developed a number of persuasive techniques based on the principles of commitment and consistency. Each of the methods described below relies on the idea that once people make a commitment, they feel both internal and external pressure to follow through.

Foot-in-the-Door Technique

The foot-in-the-door technique is named for the efforts of door-to-door salespeople to get "one foot in the door" as a tactic for getting into the house to make a sale. It is based on the idea that people who comply with small requests are more likely to do so with later, larger requests. For example, if we can persuade a difficult person to listen quietly for a few moments, this increases our likelihood of gaining his subsequent cooperation in other areas as well. The trick is to secure the person's cooperation on a small matter in a way that does not threaten his freedom of choice. The reverse, however, is also true: A person who refuses an initial request is also less likely to grant a second request. Therefore, we should be careful about what we ask for, how we ask, and when we ask.

Labeling Technique

The labeling technique of securing commitment involves, first, assigning the person a positive label and, second, requesting a favor consistent with the label. People are especially sensitive to positive labels, even when someone else assigns those labels arbitrarily. Positive labels provide people with positive reputations, which, in turn, increase the psychological pressure for them to behave in ways consistent with the labels. For example, people we label as helpful are more likely to assist us than are people we label as uncooperative. People are also more likely to comply with later requests after being labeled positively for cooperating with an earlier request.

Reciprocity

One of the most powerful, yet unspoken, rules of social behavior is reciprocity. Simply put, we have a tendency to treat others as they have treated us. We tend to respond to the positive actions of others with positive actions toward those persons, and the reverse is also true. That is, we retaliate against the negative behaviors of others toward us with negative behaviors toward them. For example, if someone speaks to us in a condescending tone, we respond in kind. On the other hand, reciprocity obligates us to repay the kind acts of others with similar kind acts of our own. Whenever people go out of their way to acknowledge us or to treat us kindly, we usually return the favor. The norm of reciprocity is the foundation of some of humankind's best moral behavior, but it is also the source of some of the worst.

We can see the norm of reciprocity at work every time we go walking or running in a public place. If we wave at other people who happen to be walking or running in the opposite direction, they will almost always wave back. If we fail to acknowledge other people, they will usually avoid acknowledging us as well. The reverse is also true: If other people acknowledge us with friendly greetings and waves, we feel compelled to return these gestures.

This means that if we want other people to treat us with respect and dignity, we should not wait to see how they behave. It is up to us, not them, to set the bar by proactively modeling positive behaviors. When we treat others with professionalism and courtesy, regardless of our personal feelings, they feel compelled to do the same.

An example of reciprocity might involve someone speaking rudely to an officer. If the officer has been courteous and respectful throughout the exchange, reciprocity allows the officer to highlight the person's bad behavior. "Sir, I don't understand why you feel it's necessary to be rude," the officer might explain. "Have I treated you with anything less than respect?" In many cases, simply pointing out a person's behavior is enough to motivate a change. Because we have behaved courteously, the person is obligated to do the same. While the rules of reciprocity are usually left unspoken, they can, nonetheless, be powerful motivators.

Door-in-the-Face Technique

The door-in-the-face technique involves making an inflated request (one that will almost certainly be rejected) and following it with a smaller request. Starting with an unrealistic request increases the likelihood that the person will accept the smaller (desired) request. For example, an officer might tell a person: "I have dozens of questions for you, but that seems like a lot to ask. So, let's not worry about that right now. Is it okay if I ask you just a couple of simple questions?" It is important to note, however, that this technique does not usually work if the first request seems completely unreasonable. Again, we need to be careful about what we ask for, how we ask, and when we ask.

Psychological Reactance

While the techniques outlined above can enhance our abilities to persuade others, each has its limits. People, especially those from individualistic cultures (such as the United States, Canada, and England), place a high value on their freedom. When a person feels his ability to choose is threatened, he will attempt to regain control, whether by simply refusing to comply or by doing exactly the opposite of what he has been asked to do. Our human tendency to resist attempts to control our freedom, known as psychological reactance, also explains why our attempts to control others often have the opposite effect. Therefore, to promote positive behavior and gain voluntary cooperation, we should avoid restricting people's freedom of choice to the point where they feel compelled to resist. In the end, it is up to each person to decide whether or not to cooperate and, if willing to cooperate, to what degree and with whom.

CLOSING THE DEAL

Thus far this chapter has addressed the importance of conflict style and language, meeting people's basic needs, allowing them to save face, and securing a commitment. Three final strategies for promoting positive behavior and gaining voluntary cooperation are to make it easy on the person, deal with only one issue at a time, and reward positive behaviors.

Make It Easy

If we want others to accept our solutions, we should make it as easy as possible for them to do so. Rather than arguing with them, we want to make their decisions as painless as possible. This begins with a shift in our focus from problems to solutions. Rather than focusing on problems, we should concentrate on solutions that are easy to accept and easy to implement. One way of accomplishing this is by emphasizing the other person's interests. Most people are simply too concerned with their own needs and interests to consider the needs of others. Framing the problem in a way that places the other person's interests first is one way of effectively removing obstacles and making it easier to reach agreement.

Less Is More

It is a fact that the more we ask for, the less we will receive. Before we ask someone to change her behavior, we should be clear (at least in our own minds) about what we want. As we have learned, we should make requests in clear, specific, behavioral terms that are easy to understand and easy to measure. We should also restrict our requests to no more than one behavior at a time. If we ask for too much, the person can become overwhelmed and may not understand what we expect from her. Simply put, the less we ask for and the more clear and specific we are with our request, the better our chances of getting what we need.

Offer Rewards

Human behavior is, at its core, the product of reinforcements and punishments. Anytime we are rewarded for performing a behavior, we are more likely to repeat the behavior in the future under similar circumstances. Conversely, if we are punished for performing an action, we are less likely to do it again. Because people are sensitive to outcomes, we should take every opportunity to reward them for appropriate behavior. If, for example, someone who is irate or emotional takes the time to listen, we should reward the effort, especially if we want the person to continue the behavior. This can be as simple as saying, "Sir, thanks for your patience and thanks for listening." Rewarding people for their efforts is one of the easiest and most effective ways to shape behavior.

On the other hand, when a person behaves inappropriately, we should challenge that behavior in a positive way. For instance: "Sir, the only way that we can better understand each other is if one person speaks at a time." Punishment, although effective under certain circumstances, should be used only as a last resort. Moreover, to be effective, we should warn the person ahead of time about the kinds of behaviors that are unacceptable and ensure that the level of punishment is appropriate. Whenever we punish without warning or punish too severely, we run the risk of resentment and resistance.

It is important to note that when we use consequences to shape another's behavior, we need to be patient. Shaping a person's behavior can be a difficult process. We must also be consistent with our applications of rewards and punishments. In other words, each time the person offers an appropriate response, we should reinforce the behavior. The same is true of punishment: It must be applied consistently and predictably. Contrary to popular belief, changing a person's behavior is a difficult and tedious undertaking. Dozens—in some cases hundreds—of applications are often required to change a person's response. However, when used appropriately, rewards and punishments can significantly enhance positive behavior in ways that might not otherwise be possible, without creating unnecessary resistance or resentment.

SUMMARY

One of our primary goals when interacting with others, especially with people who are irate, frustrated, or difficult, is to gain voluntary cooperation. Fortunately, there are a number of techniques that can assist us in achieving that goal. To begin with, we should adopt an assertive style of communication, including the use of D-E-R scripts. An assertive style allows us to express our concerns, set limits, and direct the actions of others in respectful ways. Next, we should monitor our words and language. Words are powerful. The right words spoken at the right time and in the right way can be especially effective. On the other hand, the wrong words spoken at the wrong time and in the wrong way can be disastrous. Promoting positive behavior also requires that we meet the person's basic needs, give him a stake in the process, and allow him the opportunity to save face. Finally, we should ask the person for a commitment, because we all have a strong psychological drive to maintain consistency between our words and our actions. However, anytime we solicit a person's commitment and cooperation, we should be careful not to limit his freedom to the point where he feels it necessary to attempt to regain control.

The next chapter outlines the fourth stage in the IMPACT model: Achieve rapport.

STUDY QUESTIONS

1. Why is gaining voluntary cooperation important in law enforcement?

2. Describe the three basic styles of conflict communication.

3. Explain the three components of a D-E-R script.

4. What are the differences between "you" statements and "I" statements?

5. Why is it important to honor a person's need for respect?

6. What is psychological reactance?

ACHIEVE RAPPORT

———•——

Pretend that every single person you meet has a sign around his or her neck that says, "Make me feel important."

—Mary Kay Ash

The abilities to establish and to maintain rapport are critical aspects of communicating successfully with others. Simply put, rapport is the process of building mutual liking and trust. When we have a rapport with someone, we engage naturally. We feel a sense of comfort and familiarity, we lower our barriers to resistance, and we become more receptive to the other person's ideas. The better we are at establishing and maintaining rapport, the more effective we will be at persuading others, promoting positive behavior, diagnosing problems, managing conflict, and soothing strong emotions. On the other hand, unless we can build trust and rapport, others are unlikely to share their thoughts and feelings with us, listen to our advice, or honor our requests.

We begin to build rapport with others by finding similarities and creating connections. In some cases, rapport occurs effortlessly. Connecting with the person is easy—we discover quickly that we have many interests in common, we feel naturally at ease, and we are comfortable sharing our thoughts and feelings. We listen to and validate the other person, and he listens to and validates us. In other cases, it is more difficult to build rapport. We find ourselves struggling to find common ground. Rather than connecting easily and effortlessly, we must look for ways to build rapport systematically. In either case, building rapport is an important step to successful communication and problem solving. It is also instrumental to our successful use of many of the other techniques outlined in this book.

TRUST AND RAPPORT

Research findings have consistently supported the idea that the "messenger is the message." In other words, the way we evaluate a message is a direct reflection of our perception of the person delivering the message. The more favorably we view the messenger (the person delivering the message), the more favorably we view the message itself. This is because we transfer our feelings about the messenger, whether positive or negative, to the message, a phenomenon psychologists refer to as the halo effect. As most people can attest, we are more likely to listen to messages from people we admire or respect than from individuals we dislike or disrespect. The more others like and trust us, the more apt they are to listen to, and to be influenced by, our messages. Our abilities to build trust and rapport and, in turn, our success at persuading others are influenced by first impressions, credibility, likability, and power.

First Impressions

Research has shown that in the first few milliseconds of meeting someone for the first time, we decide whether we like the person or not. The first impressions we form of others are based almost exclusively on nonverbal signals. We judge others based on their appearance, body language, demeanor, mannerisms, and dress. When we meet someone for the first time, we generally know very little about the person. Therefore, the person's physical appearance and nonverbal messages are all that we have to go on. Based on what we see, we form impressions about what the person is like and what types of behaviors to expect. Forming first impressions is not a conscious process; rather, it is something that seems to be hardwired into the human nervous system.

To complicate matters further, first impressions can be stubbornly difficult to change. This is because our first impressions (either conscious or unconscious) act as filters. They affect how we interpret and react to a person's future behavior. If our first impression of someone is negative (for example, we perceive the person as rude or condescending), we attach a negative label (such as "rude") to the person. We don't label the person as merely "having a bad day." Rather, we label her a "bad person." If a person is rude in one setting, we expect her to be rude in other settings as well. On the other hand, if our first impression of a person is positive (for example, we see her as polite or courteous), we attach a positive label (such as "polite"). Again, we don't label the person as "having a good day." Rather, we label her a "good person." If she is polite in one situation, we expect her to be polite in other situations.

Because first impressions act as filters, once we form an impression, we interpret the person's future behaviors in ways that confirm our earlier conclusions. If we have labeled a person as rude, we look for other discourteous behaviors while ignoring or discounting evidence that does not fit our expectations. When the person does something consistent with our first impression, we tell ourselves, "I knew this guy was a jerk." On the other hand, if the person behaves in a way that is inconsistent with our first impression, we ignore the evidence. "Anybody can say something nice," we might say. "This guy is still a jerk." The old adage "You have only one chance to make a good first impression" is especially important in many law enforcement settings, where we often have only one contact with any given person. By paying attention to our nonverbal messages (facial expressions, mannerisms, and appearance), we can influence the first impressions that others form of us and, in turn, increase our abilities to connect, to persuade, and to motivate others.

Credibility

The ancient Greek philosopher Aristotle invested considerable time studying how the politicians of his day managed to persuade voters. He identified credibility, or ethos, as one of the three principal methods of persuasion. Contrary to popular belief, credibility (that is, believability), is not something a person possesses, like eye color or height. Rather, it is something that can be awarded only by others; it must be earned. Aristotle further identified three factors that affect a person's credibility: competence (or expertise), character (trustworthiness), and goodwill. Competence involves how much we know—in other words, the type and amount of expertise we possess. One measure of competence that is often overlooked is physical appearance. As a general rule, the more knowledgeable, competent, and attractive we appear to be, the greater our ability to persuade others.

The second factor in credibility, character, encompasses the traits commonly associated with trustworthiness, such as dependability, integrity, and fairness. It also includes our beliefs about whether someone is communicating honestly and openly. We rate people whom we believe to be honest, fair, and open as trustworthy. On the other hand, we view people whom we consider to be dishonest with suspicion.

The third characteristic, goodwill, involves the extent to which we believe someone has our best interests in mind. Most of us prefer to interact with others we see as honest, authentic, and transparent. Conversely, we tend to judge people with hidden agendas more harshly, especially if we believe they are attempting to hide something from us.

Likability

The third element influencing the ability to establish rapport is likability. We are all more likely to be persuaded by people we like than by those we dislike. As Dale Carnegie (1936/1981) observes in his classic book *How to Win Friends and Influence People,* liking and persuasion are inseparable. One important aspect of liking is similarity—that is, the degree to which we believe others are similar to us in their interests and beliefs. Our preference for similarity seems to hold whether it involves opinions, values, personality traits, backgrounds, or lifestyles. In other words, people like people who are like themselves. This means that we can enhance our ability to connect with others by communicating that "we are alike." While this might seem challenging considering the spectrum of personalities and attitudes that law enforcement officers inevitably encounter, it is usually not as difficult as it might appear. We can almost always find similarities and common interests with others if we are willing to work at it long enough.

One way of demonstrating interest is to focus on the other person and his needs. We do this by listening actively to the person and to his behavior, by identifying key words and phrases, and by looking for similarities. It is worth noting, however, that just as similarities can enhance our abilities to communicate and to connect with others, dissimilarities often have the opposite effect—that is, they make it more difficult to establish trust and rapport.

Power

The fourth aspect of establishing rapport is power, or the ability to influence others. Power can be divided into two categories: positional and personal. Positional power is determined by our status, rank, or authority, which includes our abilities to reward and to punish others for their behaviors. For example, a supervisor has more positional power than a subordinate employee. Personal power, on the other hand, has to do with individual characteristics such as knowledge, expertise, determination, courage, and communication skills. While positional power is determined by a person's standing within an organization's structure, personal power is awarded by others because they respect or admire the person. Thus, the amount of personal power someone possesses has nothing to do with rank or authority; rather, it is based solely on the person's character and competence.

Some people have considerable positional power but very little personal power. For example, a supervisor may have extensive formal authority—including the abilities to reward and to punish the behaviors of others—but may lack personal power because subordinate employees do not respect him. Other people possess little, if any, positional power but still have considerable personal influence over others. In law enforcement this is often the case with peer-group leaders, officers who possess little formal authority but wield significant influence because of their tenure, expertise, or other personal factors.

As law enforcement officers, we have considerable positional power. We have the authority to carry firearms, seize people and their belongings, and arrest those suspected of violating the law. Unfortunately, too many officers rely solely on positional power to compel compliance. Rather than ask, they demand. Although this can be effective in the short term, it often creates more problems than it solves. People follow such orders by doing only the minimum required. In other cases, they may do the opposite or refuse to follow orders altogether.

While there are clearly times when it is necessary to use positional power, we should do so only as a last resort. Instead, we should work to develop our personal power. Unlike positional power, there are no restrictions on personal power. Indeed, our personal power actually increases the more frequently and effectively we use it. The more we develop our knowledge, experience, communication skills, and other desirable traits, the more powerful we become.

INTERPERSONAL COMMUNICATION

The next facet of building rapport is our ability to communicate effectively. As noted in Chapter 1, we continuously send and receive messages whenever we interact with others. While some of those messages are clearly intentional—that is, meant to transmit information, invoke a response, or both—others are sent without conscious awareness. However, regardless of our intent, all behavior communicates something valuable about our thoughts, feelings, and attitudes.

The messages that we send to others can be divided into two general categories: verbal and nonverbal. Verbal communication consists of the words we use to transmit information, while nonverbal communication entails those parts of a message sent without words, such as facial expressions, gaze, tone of voice, proxemics, gestures, and posture. Research by psychologist Albert Mehrabian (1972) suggests that 93% of a message's emotional impact is derived from nonverbal sources. In contrast, only 7% of a message's emotional value is contained in the actual words that are used (see Figure 5.1).

Even without special training, most people are fairly skilled at decoding many types of nonverbal messages. This means that anytime we communicate with others, especially people who are irate, frustrated, or emotional, we need to be careful about the signals we send, especially nonverbal cues. This includes ensuring that our words and behaviors send the same message.

Verbal Messages

The words we use constitute our verbal messages. Most messages contain both emotional and logical dimensions. The emotional dimension entails the communication of feelings (anger, sadness, or disgust, for example), attitudes (whether we like or dislike something

Figure 5.1 Emotional Impact of Communicative Modalities

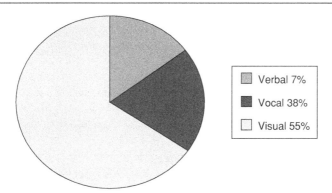

Verbal 7%
Vocal 38%
Visual 55%

SOURCE: Adapted from Mehrabian, A. (1972). *Nonverbal communication.* New Brunswick, NJ: Aldine Transaction.

or someone), and predispositions (such as anxiousness or confidence). Clearly, some ideas are difficult or uncomfortable to put into words and, therefore, are best expressed nonverbally. The logical dimension of messages, on the other hand, represents the communication of thoughts or ideas and relies heavily on the spoken word.

Unlike with other less conscious aspects of communication, we have the power to choose our words. The language we select can significantly influence our ability to establish rapport. The right words can go a long way toward enhancing trust, improving communication, and promoting positive behavior. Conversely, the wrong words can destroy any chance we may have of connecting with others. In choosing our words, we should consider the following elements:

- *Greeting:* Anytime we contact someone, we should acknowledge the person with a greeting, such as "Good morning" or "Hi, are you the person who called?"

- *Introduction:* In addition to greeting the person, we should begin every contact by introducing ourselves and by explaining the nature of our business. A simple introduction should include name, title, agency, and reason for the contact. For instance: "Good afternoon, I am Officer Jackson with the Pleasantville Police Department. Can I speak with you about your neighbor?"

- *Use of proper title:* Except where it is obviously unnecessary because of an existing relationship, we should initially address the person by using the appropriate title as well as name. Until we have obtained the person's permission to use a less formal form of address, we should address the person as "Sir" or "Ma'am."

- *Use of person's name:* Addressing a person by name demonstrates personal concern. It shows that we have taken the time to learn and remember the person's name. This can be an important step in establishing trust and rapport. Nonetheless, there are times when calling a person by his first name is inappropriate. If there is any doubt as to the appropriateness of using someone's first name, we should ask permission. For example, "Mr. Johnson, is it all right if I call you Steve?"

- *Use of polite and respectful language:* Regardless of what the other person does or says, we should remain professional and polite at all times. Simple phrases such as "thank you" and "you're welcome" are considered basic civilities. Failure to use these phrases is often considered rude or impolite.

- *Use of proper language:* We should try to use language that is easily and commonly understood. We should avoid using technical terms, police jargon, and other phrases that are unique to law enforcement when explaining things to people outside the law enforcement community. For example, "Sir, I understand that you are having a problem with your neighbor" is more likely to be understood than "Sir, I was dispatched to investigate a possible civil action against your neighbor."

- *Small talk:* Engaging in some friendly small talk or chitchat usually costs nothing but a few moments of time and can go a long way toward establishing rapport and humanizing the encounter. Not engaging in small talk when appropriate can appear callous or uncaring. There is more to interpersonal communication than "just the facts."

Vocal Messages

The term *paralanguage* refers to nonverbal vocal messages such as the rate, volume, pitch, tone, and cadence of speech. We use paralanguage to reinforce messages, to shape impressions, and to regulate our interactions with others. Our messages can take on different meanings depending on the vocal qualities of rate, volume, pitch, tone, and cadence, as well as the words we choose to emphasize. Because paralanguage can be difficult to control, it often provides important information about our true feelings and attitudes. More important, studies have found that when our paralanguage contradicts our spoken words, people tend to pay more attention to the paralanguage and other nonverbal cues than to our verbal messages. In other words, it is not always what we say that matters, but rather how we say it. This also suggests that to communicate effectively with others, we must ensure that our verbal and nonverbal messages are consistent. We should be aware of the following aspects of our vocal messages:

- *Consistency of paralanguage and words:* Our paralanguage should always match our spoken words. If we tell a person that we are concerned about her problem but our tone is harsh or critical, we send conflicting messages. If we say that we are concerned, our tone should demonstrate an appropriate level of empathy.
- *Appropriate volume:* Low to moderate volume levels are typically best for interpersonal communication. When we bark out orders or yell at others, we are seen as unprofessional or, in some cases, out of control. Very few behaviors demonstrate self-assurance as well as "quiet confidence."
- *Appropriate speech:* With a few rare exceptions, our tone of voice should be calm and professional. There is never a good reason to use sarcasm or derogatory language. Not only is such language unprofessional, but its use also undermines trust and rapport.

Visual Messages

Nonverbal messages are especially important because what we do is often more meaningful than what we say. If, for example, we tell a person that we are interested in better understanding his story while we look at our watch and roll our eyes, we communicate disinterest. In most cases, people look at nonverbal gestures (such as looking at our watch and rolling our eyes) as unvarnished indicators of our true feeling and react accordingly.

Facial Expressions

Anytime we interact with others, we pay special attention to their faces for signs of emotion, interest, and attitude. We use our faces to regulate our interactions with others, to send uncomfortable messages, and to reinforce or to modify verbal messages. Studies further suggest that facial expressions offer unique insight into people's true emotional states. Indeed, some researchers have gone so far as to suggest that the study of the face is the study of emotion itself. As early as 1872, in his book *The Expression of the Emotions in Man and Animals,* Charles Darwin (1872/1998) discussed the important role of the face in expressing emotion. Darwin believed that our ability to communicate nonverbally evolved in the same ways as the rest of the brain and body. Long before human beings mastered verbal messages, primates used facial expressions to transmit their attitudes and emotions.

Psychologist Paul Ekman (2003) has identified six universal facial expressions of emotion (anger, disgust, fear, joy, surprise, and sadness) and the distinct positions of the eyebrows, forehead, eyes, and mouth associated with each expression. For example, happiness and surprise are noticeable in the eyes and lower face, while anger is visible in the lower face, eyebrows, and forehead. Although faces can transmit a wealth of important information, they can be difficult to read accurately. This is because our faces transmit two sets of signals: the voluntary messages that we want others to see and the involuntary expressions that we prefer to hide. Facial expressions can also change very quickly (in as little as one-tenth of a second in some cases). Therefore, to read faces accurately, we must learn to pay special attention to the areas around the eyebrows, forehead, eyes, and mouth. With enough practice, anyone can learn to pick out even the subtlest expressions with astonishing accuracy.

Posture

Our posture provides important clues about our desire to be closer, both physically and psychologically, to people we like. Posture consists of two primary dimensions: immediacy and relaxation. Immediacy is observable primarily in relationships. It communicates our feelings of warmth as well as our desire to be closer to others. We demonstrate our attitudes toward others through approach and avoidance behaviors. Approach behaviors include direct body orientation, symmetric positioning, and a forward lean. In contrast, avoidance behaviors, actions that signal dislike or disinterest, involve leaning away, poor eye contact, and a closed posture. The second dimension of posture, relaxation, is influenced by status differences among people. As a general rule, we tend to exhibit more relaxed posture in nonthreatening environments (when interacting with others in status positions similar to or lower than ours) and less relaxed posture when we feel threatened (when interacting with others in higher status positions).

Understanding posture is important in building rapport because we tend to increase approach behaviors and adapt a more relaxed posture around people we like or admire. Conversely, we are more likely to increase avoidance behaviors and to show signs of tension around people we dislike. Generally, we face people we like directly, while we face away from the people we dislike. People often interpret closed posture as a sign of dislike and disinterest. On the other hand, an open and relaxed posture is commonly believed to be a sign of liking and interest.

Proxemics

Like other animals, human beings claim and stake out spaces to call their own. Proxemics, the study of how people and animals use space to communicate, consists of two major dimensions: distance and territoriality. Distance is the actual physical space between people. One way that we communicate our feelings toward others is by controlling the physical space around us. Territoriality involves the claiming of an area. Animals claim and defend territory for a variety of reasons, including food and mating. Humans also engage in territorial behavior as a way of demonstrating their power and status.

According to anthropologist Edward Hall (1966), our choices regarding personal space—that is, the particular distances we maintain from others—depend on how we feel about the other persons. Hall identifies four distances, or zones, that we use to control our interaction with others. The first distance, the intimate zone, is our personal space. It represents our innermost region of interaction, typically in the space ranging from physical contact to about 18 inches from the body. This zone is reserved for the few special people in our lives. The second area, the personal zone, extends from 18 inches to around 4 feet out from the body. This is the distance we prefer when conversing with friends and close acquaintances. The third region, the social zone, ranges from 4 feet to about 8 feet out. We use the social zone to conduct business or when talking with others in a professional capacity. The final area, the public zone, begins at around 10 feet from the body and extends indefinitely. At this distance, communication tends to be formal, such as a public speech.

When someone violates our personal space, the experience can be either positive or negative, depending on our feelings for the person. For example, if somebody we like sits closer to us than expected (positive violation), we usually do not mind. In contrast, if a person we dislike comes too close (negative violation), we often feel anxious or uncomfortable. The outcome in either case depends on our relationship with the person. The distances that we maintain from others, as well as the distances that they maintain from us, communicate important information about our feelings and attitudes. With proxemics, as with other forms of nonverbal communication, we should monitor the messages that we send to others to promote an image of professionalism, warmth, and respect whenever possible.

Eye Contact

Eye contact is usually the first form of interaction we have with another person. If that exchange is negative, we often have no further contact. We also use eye contact to express emotion and to decrease the physical and psychological distance between others and ourselves. Eye contact is perhaps most important in communicating liking and interest. We tend to gaze more at things and people we find likable or interesting and to avoid eye contact with people we dislike. This makes eye contact a simple yet effective way of demonstrating interest in others. Failure to establish positive eye contact, on the other hand, can signal our disapproval or disliking of others, significantly reducing our abilities to establish rapport, build trust, and open lines of communication.

Nonverbal Behavior Strategies

The messages that we send to others are affected not only by the words we choose but also by our facial expressions, gaze, posture, and proxemics. The following strategies can help us send the most consistent, effective messages possible, while helping to establish trust and rapport:

- *Visual and vocal accord:* One function of nonverbal communication is to clarify verbal messages. As we have seen, perhaps the most important aspect of body language is that it matches our verbal message. When our verbal and visual messages are inconsistent, people are more likely to believe the nonverbal message.

- *Open posture:* One of the most obvious expressions of nonverbal behavior is posture. We should monitor our posture at all times, maintaining an open posture whenever possible and without compromising officer safety. An open posture typically involves relaxed arms and shoulders, appropriate eye contact, positive facial expression, and frontal orientation. Presenting such a posture is one of the simplest displays of nonverbal communication we can control, although it may initially require some conscious effort.

- *Body alignment:* Whenever possible and without compromising officer safety, we should adopt a frontal orientation. A severely angled or bladed posture communicates defensiveness. Obviously, in higher-risk situations, tactical stances may be necessary and entirely appropriate.

- *Positive facial expression:* As we communicate with others we focus naturally on their faces. Facial expressions communicate a great deal about our feelings, attitudes, and interests. Because communication is oriented to the face, positive facial expressions are among the most important aspects of nonverbal communication. Lowered eyebrows and tight lips are two indicators of anger and should be avoided.

- *Positive eye contact:* While too much eye contact can be seen as confrontational or rude, appropriate eye contact is usually viewed as an indicator of sincerity and attentiveness. People who do not make eye contact are often viewed as deceptive or untrustworthy. As a general rule, we should engage people in strong, positive eye contact for no more than a few seconds at a time before looking away. We should continue with this pattern throughout the interaction.

- *Appropriate distance:* When interacting with citizens who do not present a threat to officer safety, we should remain in a zone approximately 2 to 5 feet away. Standing too close to a person may be offensive, while maintaining too great a distance communicates disinterest or dislike.

- *Suitable gestures:* People can become unsettled when someone uses overly broad and expansive gestures. During normal interaction with others, we should consider keeping our gestures within a "box" that is roughly the same area as our torso. Pointing at someone with one's finger is usually considered rude and inappropriate. Using a flashlight or other object to point with only aggravates an already inappropriate gesture.

- *Smiling as appropriate:* A smile is an effective way of disarming a person's natural defenses and can go a long way toward establishing trust and rapport. While smiling is clearly inappropriate to certain law enforcement contacts, there is no reason that law enforcement officers should be viewed as "unsmiling" automatons, interested in "just the facts." People smile at each other in a variety of contexts, and there is no reason, given an appropriate set of circumstances, that we should not do the same.

- *Mirroring as appropriate:* We can help to build rapport by mirroring, or reflecting, the other person's communication, including voice tone, cadence, and volume, as well as other nonverbal messages, such as body positioning, facial expressions, and gaze. It can also be useful to mirror the kinds of words the person uses. For example, some people tend to use words that reflect visual processing ("Do you see what I mean?"), while others favor words related to auditory ("Do you hear me?") or kinesthetic ("Do you feel me?") processing. The basic principle of mirroring is that when the other person sees us, he sees himself, which most people find highly attractive. Mirroring is generally most effective when it occurs subtly. Therefore, we should avoid overly explicit attempts to mirror a person's words or behaviors.

SUMMARY

Building trust and rapport is critical to successful communication. When we have rapport with someone, we engage naturally. We feel comfortable sharing our thoughts, feelings, and concerns. Establishing rapport begins with finding similarities and creating connections. In some cases, rapport occurs naturally—we discover quickly that we have many interests in common with the other person. In other cases, we must look for ways to build rapport systematically. Our abilities to establish and to maintain rapport are influenced by first impressions, credibility, likability, and power. Our capacity to develop trust and rapport also depends on our ability to communicate effectively with others.

One aspect of communication that studies have found to be especially important is nonverbal communication, including eye contact, posture, proxemics, gestures, and facial expressions. This is because what we do is often more important than what we say.

We continuously send and receive messages whenever we interact with others. While some of these messages are intentional—that is, meant to transmit information, invoke a response, or both—others are sent without conscious awareness. Regardless of our intent, all of our behavior communicates something important about our thoughts and feelings. Even without the benefit of specialized training, most people are relatively skilled at decoding many types of nonverbal messages. Anytime we interact with others, we need to be careful about the types of messages—especially nonverbal messages—that we send. This includes ensuring that our verbal, vocal, and visual signals are consistent.

The next chapter details the fifth step of the IMPACT model: Control your response.

STUDY QUESTIONS

1. What is rapport?
2. What is meant by the phrase "The messenger is the message"?
3. List three elements that influence the building of trust and rapport.
4. According to research findings published by psychologist Albert Mehrabian, how much of a message's emotional impact is the result of nonverbal communication?
5. What is paralanguage? Why is an understanding of paralanguage important to effective interpersonal communication?
6. List three types of visual messages.

⋇ 6 ⋇

CONTROL YOUR RESPONSE

———•◦•———

There is nothing either good or bad, but thinking makes it so.
—William Shakespeare

None of us, regardless of our law enforcement tenure or experience, are immune to emotions. We are subject to the same kinds of frustration, anger, irritation, hostility, fear, and depression as everyone else. While emotions perform a number of important functions, strong feelings can create a host of problems: They can interfere with our ability to listen, make it difficult for us to concentrate, and lead to aggressive behavior. Considering the range of irate, frustrated, and difficult people that law enforcement officers encounter on a daily basis, there will almost certainly be times when we will find ourselves overwhelmed by strong emotions. When this happens, we have two choices: We can control our emotions, or we can allow our emotions to control us. Anytime we allow our emotions to control us, we become part of the problem rather than part of the solution. As law enforcement professionals, we simply don't have the luxury of surrendering ourselves to strong emotions. The costs of anger, frustration, and hostility are simply too high. Rather, we must master the self-awareness and emotional management skills necessary to control our response.

As we learned previously, our lives are influenced by two mental systems: one emotional, the other logical. The first system, the emotional "go" system, is concerned primarily with the emotional significance of people and things, particularly fear-related stimuli. It continuously scans the environment for threats and, at the first sign of danger, activates the body's stress response ("fight or flight"). The second system, the neutral "no" system, is emotionally objective. It is a consequence of the rational brain and is responsible for the higher-order functions of logic, planning, and language, as well as for modifying the duration and intensity of our emotional responses. Which brain system is currently in charge is determined by the reticular activating system (RAS), a kind of "toggle switch" located in an area beginning at the top of the brain stem and continuing into the cerebral cortex. The RAS switches brain systems at two different times: when we become emotionally aroused and when we relax. When we become emotionally charged, the RAS shuts down the cerebral cortex, allowing the emotional brain to assume control. Once the threat has passed, the RAS switches the cortex back on, letting us regain access to our logical brain.

The two systems—the emotional "go" system and the neutral "no" system—are connected by a collection of nerves that link thinking with feeling. These connections also allow the brain to control the rest of the body by regulating our physiological systems, including the autonomic nervous system and the endocrine system. Due to our unique abilities to use and understand language, we humans are the only organisms capable of thinking ourselves into an emotional state. By simply thinking hard enough about something frightening, we can increase our heart rate, intensify our breathing, and dilate our pupils. Because our thoughts can produce measurable physiological changes, the first step in managing our emotions is to manage the language that we use to label people and events.

Most experts agree that we have only two options for managing emotions: We can change the environment, or we can change our response. As law enforcement professionals, we are often unable to control our environment. We are dispatched to calls for service and summoned for assistance by forces beyond our control. In most cases we have no choice but to respond, and once on scene we have no choice but to handle events to conclusion, even when we feel ourselves overcome with strong emotions. When we are unable to change the environment, we have only one option left: We must change our response.

THE TRUTH ABOUT ANGER

Three common myths about anger influence many of our emotional responses. All of these myths have been repeated so many times that some have assumed an air of legitimacy. Some of the misinformation feeding these myths can be traced to early theories in psychology; other beliefs about anger are the products of childhood experiences. Regardless of how we acquire our beliefs, they influence the ways we think about and respond to anger in a number of important ways. By understanding the truth about anger, we will be better able to manage our emotions in positive, productive ways that allow us to be part of the solution rather than part of the problem.

Myth 1: Other People Are Responsible for My Anger

The first myth is that others are responsible for our frustration, anger, and hostility. According to this view, we do little more than respond to the behavior of others, similar to a puppet operated by a set of strings. The puppeteer pulls a string and we become angry. The puppeteer pulls a different string and we become happy. Other people are somehow to blame for our emotions. This belief is perhaps best expressed by the statement "You made me mad!" Despite the popularity of this view, nothing could be further from the truth. We are responsible for our emotions. Nobody can make us angry. Nobody can make us happy. We choose anger and hostility in the same ways that we choose happiness or joy. What we feel, how intensely we feel it, and whether or not we act on those feelings are choices.

Myth 2: Expressing Anger Is Healthy

The idea that expressing anger is healthy stems from the historical view of anger as a form of catharsis—that is, a way of reducing stress and unhealthy emotions. The problem is that each time we respond with anger, we practice anger. We are, at our core, creatures of habit. Not surprisingly, much of how we respond emotionally and behaviorally is the product of conditioning. We develop habits, or automatic ways of responding, by repeatedly practicing the same patterns of thoughts and behaviors. In other words, the more we practice anger, the more likely we are to respond with anger in the future.

**Myth 3: My Only Choices Are to Express
My Feelings or to Hold Them In**

Many people believe that there are only two ways of managing
negative emotions: We can release our anger, hostility, and aggression
on others, or we can hold those feelings in. Despite the long-standing
acceptance of this belief, it is simply not true. There is a third choice.
By improving our self-awareness and emotional intelligence, we can
tone down or modify our emotions, much as we can turn down the heat
on a pot of boiling water. We can do this by identifying and modifying
unhealthy beliefs and labels. Additionally, we can adopt an assertive
style of communication to help us set appropriate boundaries without
ignoring the interests of others.

We can draw three conclusions from the debunking of these myths:

- We are responsible for our anger.
- We can control our anger and other negative emotions.
- Poor emotional management skills have serious negative consequences.

THOUGHTS, FEELINGS, AND BEHAVIORS

Too often, the first casualty of an encounter with a difficult person is
our objectivity. An uncooperative citizen makes a nasty remark and
we respond with an equally caustic comment. This type of "eye for
an eye" thinking typically results in an unproductive cycle of action
and reaction that continues unabated until constructive dialogue is no
longer possible. While we might win the battle, too often we lose the
war. Tit-for-tat tactics seldom accomplish anything; rather, they alien-
ate others, generate complaints, and damage public trust. Effectively
managing the emotions of others begins with effectively managing our
own emotional response. If we want to be successful with irate, frustrated, and difficult people, we must first learn to identify and manage
our frustration and hostility.

All of our experiences as human beings consist of some combination of thoughts, feelings, and behaviors. Because the parts of
the brain responsible for thinking are connected to the areas of the
brain responsible for physiology, emotion, and behavior, we have

Figure 6.1 Relationship Between Thoughts, Feelings, and Behaviors

the ability to control our emotions and behaviors by controlling our thoughts. Simply put, our thinking has a direct influence on how we feel and how we behave. This means that the ways we think about people and things are important determinants of our responses. Unfortunately, most of us are largely unaware of the ways our thoughts influence our emotions and behaviors. We are also largely naive about the beliefs, self-talk statements, and labels that occupy much of our thinking.

Many of our beliefs, self-talk statements, and labels develop early in life, long before we are aware of their importance. As children, we develop beliefs based on our experiences with parents, teachers, and peers. Young children are acutely aware of behavioral reinforcements and punishments. Behaviors that are rewarded and reinforced are more likely to be repeated, while behaviors that are punished are less likely to occur again. Anytime we express anger, either as a child or as an adult, and that behavior gets us what we want, it becomes more likely that we will respond with anger in the future.

Proponents of rational emotive behavioral therapy maintain that people and things have no intrinsic emotional value. Rather, our thinking is mostly responsible for our frustration, anger, and other negative emotions toward people and things. The three-step model proposed by psychologist Albert Ellis, described below, illustrates the relationship between events, beliefs, and emotional responses.

A: Activating Event

An activating event (A) is a person or thing that acts as a stressor. It could be a motorist who refuses to sign a citation, a citizen who "pays your salary," or a supervisor who wants things done a certain way. In either case, the event triggers our appraisal, including our beliefs and self-talk statements.

B: Beliefs and Self-Talk

We use beliefs and silent self-talk statements (B) to evaluate the person or event. Some of our beliefs are rational and positive. They help us cope with frustration and soothe negative emotions. In contrast, other beliefs and self-talk statements are irrational and negative. They frequently lead to frustration and anxiety. In either case, it is the automatic nature of our beliefs and self-talk that makes them so powerful.

C: Consequences

Consequences (C), including emotions and behaviors, result from our beliefs and self-talk statements. Depending on the beliefs and statements involved, our emotional consequences can range from frustration and anger to patience and satisfaction. Behavioral consequences, such as violence and aggression, may also occur.

The commonsense view of anger is the belief that we have little or no ability to control our emotions and behaviors (see Figure 6.2). Rather, people and things are to blame for our responses. This type of A-caused-C thinking is reflected in statements like "That idiot really pissed me off!" This, however, is simply not the case. In fact, it is not the other person, or "idiot," who is responsible for the officer's emotional distress; rather, it is the officer's own labels, beliefs, and self-talk statements (see Figure 6.3). Although it is clearly impossible to eliminate all negative emotions, we can still influence the duration and intensity of our responses by challenging our irrational beliefs and labels.

The fact that we can control our emotions by monitoring our thoughts is good news. It means that if we can learn to control our beliefs, labels, and self-talk, we can better control our emotions and behaviors. This is because, contrary to conventional wisdom, the activating events in our lives are neutral. In other words, people and things have no inherent emotional value. The only value they hold is the value we assign. Because the labels we select influence our emotions and

Figure 6.2 Commonsense View of Emotions

A   C

Activating Event   Consequences (behaviors, emotions)

SOURCE: Adapted from Clark, L. (1998). *SOS help for emotions: Managing anxiety, anger, and depression.* Bowling Green, KY: Parents Press.

Figure 6.3 Correct Model of Emotions

A   B   C

Activating   Beliefs, Labels,   Consequences
Event   and Self-Talk   (behaviors, emotions)

SOURCE: Adapted from Clark, L. (1998). *SOS help for emotions: Managing anxiety, anger, and depression.* Bowling Green, KY: Parents Press.

behaviors, we have the power to choose different responses simply by selecting different labels.

BELIEFS, LABELS, AND SELF-TALK

Psychologists have identified three types of cognitions that have impacts on our emotions and behaviors: beliefs, labels, and self-talk statements. By improving our abilities to manage our beliefs and self-talk, we can learn to manage our emotions and behaviors when it matters most—that is, when we are dealing with others who are irate, frustrated, or emotional. Learning to manage our emotions will also make us more effective at connecting with others, managing conflict, and solving problems.

Beliefs

We all have beliefs about the ways we should be treated, how others should behave, and what is fair. These beliefs are especially salient when we are dealing with irate, frustrated, or difficult people. We tend to have particularly strong beliefs about the ways that we, as law enforcement professionals, should be spoken to and should be treated. Some of our beliefs are rational and lead to appropriate emotional responses.

For example, we might hold a belief that it is all right for a person who is emotionally upset to raise her voice. Our rational beliefs help us cope effectively with difficult situations and people. However, we may hold other beliefs that are irrational and harmful. Rather than helping us better control our response, they exacerbate negative emotions. For instance, we may believe that people should respect our authority at all times and regardless of their emotional state. Obviously, there will be times when otherwise intelligent, rational people will not respond to our authority. The very nature of strong emotions can make it difficult for people to reason, much less to demonstrate unquestioning respect for authority.

Four types of beliefs that can be especially harmful are should/must thinking, all-or-nothing thinking, awfulizing or maximizing, and "why" questions.

Should/Must Thinking

Should/must thinking occurs when we place demands on people and things; it is associated with words like "never," "always," and "have to." When we engage in should/must thinking, we escalate our wishes and preferences to demands. We may become emotionally upset, for example, when a person fails to demonstrate an appropriate level of respect or when a person fails to comply with a direct order. One problem with should/must thinking is that other people rarely see the world in the same ways we do. Their rules and beliefs can be different from ours. Absent obvious officer safety concerns, the key to changing our irrational beliefs is realizing that many of our rules are based on preferences and choices, not categorical imperatives. While we all have preferences for certain behaviors, there are very few absolutes.

All-or-Nothing Thinking

We engage in all-or-nothing thinking when we evaluate people and things in absolute terms. In other words, things are good or bad, positive or negative, right or wrong. There is simply nothing in between, no middle ground, no gray area. Most of us recognize that few things in life are completely "good" or completely "bad." For example, it's rare that someone is "always" a jerk or that someone "never" cooperates. The key to changing this type of thinking is to challenge the underlying rules responsible for our beliefs. Is it realistic to believe that everyone, everywhere, and every time must treat us with the utmost respect? Or might there be times when our job requires us to work with difficult people? Considering the nature of police work, there will almost certainly be times when we will be forced to work with irate, frustrated, and emotional people. The sooner we accept that fact, the sooner we can adopt healthy, realistic beliefs and take control of our emotions.

Awfulizing or Maximizing

Awfulizing or maximizing occurs when we exaggerate a minor problem into something more serious. It is associated with statements like "This is terrible!" or "This is awful!" For example, an officer who labels his contact with a difficult citizen as "the worst day in months" is likely to talk himself into a negative emotional state. The best way to challenge this form of thinking is to realize that very few things are truly "awful" or "horrible"; they are merely inconvenient. Anytime we discover ourselves awfulizing, we should immediately replace that terminology with more reasonable, emotionally cool descriptors, such as "inconvenient" or "unpleasant."

"Why" Questions

The final type of irrational belief is actually a disguised form of should/must thinking. It occurs when we repeat the same question—usually beginning with "why" or "how could"—over and over. This type of thinking is associated with questions such as "Why is this happening?" and "How could this occur?" For instance, an officer who asks, "Why do I have to deal with this idiot?" is likely to talk herself into a bad mood. Because we label the event as unfair, we refuse to accept responsibility or to deal with the consequences. Simply answering the question is one of the best ways to challenge "why" thinking. This allows us to evaluate the question logically, acknowledge the reality of the situation, and take appropriate action.

Table 6.1   Beliefs and Self-Talk Statements

Dysfunctional, Unhealthy Beliefs and Self-Talk	Results (unpleasant and unhealthy responses)
"He can't talk to me like that!"	Anger, frustration, arousal
"Who does this guy think he is?"	Anger, frustration, arousal
"I'll show this idiot who is in charge."	Anger, frustration, arousal

Functional, Healthy Beliefs and Self-Talk	Results (unpleasant but healthy responses)
"This guy must be having a bad day."	Irritation
"This guy is angry, but getting upset won't help."	Annoyance
"This is frustrating, but it's not worth getting angry."	Concern

SOURCE: Adapted from McKay, M., Rogers, P. D., & McKay, J. (1989). *When anger hurts: Quieting the storm*. Oakland, CA: New Harbinger.

Labels

Human beings are not neutral observers. We label virtually everyone and everything that we encounter. We label people and things that help us move closer to a goal as positive. Conversely, we label anyone or anything that prevents us from reaching a goal as negative, especially irate, difficult, or hostile people. We learned many of our labels during early childhood, and, like other irrational beliefs, they have become unconscious habits. Like all forms of self-talk, the labels we select act as emotional filters. While it is easy to label somebody a "jerk," we seldom realize that doing so can influence our emotions and behaviors in a host of negative ways. The trick to correcting negative labels is to ask ourselves whether they are truly accurate. For example, is a motorist who is upset about receiving a speeding ticket truly behaving like a "jerk," or is he simply being difficult because he is concerned about his insurance rates? Because labels are powerful, we should periodically check the accuracy of our labels, as well as the effects those labels have on our emotions and behaviors.

Self-Talk

Internal dialogue, or self-talk, is the real-time conversation that we have with ourselves about what is occurring in our lives. Whether we realize it or not, we engage in a continuous internal dialogue that reflects our beliefs and labels. Self-talk is what we say to ourselves about the people, events, and things that we encounter. Most of us have engaged in self-talk for so long that we are not even aware we are doing it. Our self-talk can be either positive or negative, and it is one of the major influences on how we respond emotionally and behaviorally to others. Self-talk can heat up our emotional response or it can cool it down, depending on the language that we choose. A statement like "This guy is a real idiot!" is almost certain to heat up our emotional response, while saying "This guy must be having a really bad day" is more likely to cool our reaction.

While we develop many of our labels, beliefs, and self-talk statements during early childhood, many of these patterns continue unchallenged throughout our adult lives. If we continue to use the same irrational labels, beliefs, and statements long enough, they become patterns—that is, automatic ways of responding to people and things without any conscious awareness of the process or consequences. The fact that most of us are unaware of our self-talk is one of the main reasons that negative patterns develop and take root. Fortunately, early childhood conditioning is not fate. With a little effort, we can change the habits that we acquired early in life.

In the end, there is nothing automatic about anger or hostility. It all comes down to choice. We choose what to think about and we choose what not to think about. We have control over the content of our minds. Anytime we find strong emotions getting in the way of our personal or professional effectiveness, we can, and should, identify and challenge our irrational and unhealthy thoughts before they become habits. We also need to replace our irrational beliefs with more realistic cognitions.

STEPS TO IMPROVING EMOTIONAL MANAGEMENT

Anger and other caustic emotions can damage relationships, undermine public trust, and reduce officer safety. Moreover, anger and hostility are not very effective at facilitating communication and problem solving. Now that we have a better understanding of emotions, as well as the roles played by irrational beliefs, labels, and self-talk, we can use the following strategies to recognize and manage our reactions.

Recognize the Signs

The first step in controlling anger, hostility, and other negative emotions is to recognize the physical and mental cues. Because strong emotions produce noticeable bodily sensations and shifts in thinking, the better we are at recognizing these changes, the more successful we will be at managing our responses. The key to recognizing emotions, particularly negative emotions, is learning to diagnose the changes early, including the following:

- Elevated heart rate, respiration, and blood pressure
- Flushing
- Elevated body temperature
- Agitation
- Difficulty concentrating
- Muscle tension, especially in the shoulders, neck, and back
- Strong impulse to act
- Nausea

Once we understand the cognitive and physiological changes that accompany strong emotions, we will be better able to recognize the early signs of emotional distress. Strong emotions cause the release of adrenaline, cortisol, and other bodily chemicals, which take time to dissipate. If necessary, we may need to step away from the situation for a few moments—or minutes—until our thoughts and physiology return to normal. In this case, forewarned is forearmed. The earlier we can diagnose signs of emotion, the earlier we can intervene and the more effective our intervention is likely to be.

Take Responsibility

Once we become aware of a strong emotional response, the next step is to take responsibility. This is in direct conflict with our natural tendency to blame our negative emotions and hostility on others, arguably the main reason that we feel justified in our anger. When somebody else is responsible, we do not need to worry about changing ourselves or about the consequences of our actions. Fortunately, every situation offers a choice. Although we may not always be able to choose our circumstances, we can always choose our responses. Once we realize the ways thoughts and language shape our emotions, we can no longer blame our bad behavior on others. Managing our emotions and behaviors effectively means assuming responsibility for our thoughts, including our beliefs, labels, and self-talk statements, as well as the consequences of our actions.

Make a Proper Appraisal

The third step focuses specifically on the appraisal process. The ways that we think about events and people significantly influence our abilities to manage our emotional and behavioral responses effectively. People and things have no intrinsic emotional value. Our emotions and behaviors are not caused by objects or people but by our beliefs, labels, and self-talk. Because all emotions start with essentially the same state of general arousal, the specific emotion that we experience has more to do with how we evaluate things than with those things themselves. In fact, people often vary widely in their reactions to the same event mostly because they differ in the appraisal process.

Identify Hot Buttons

We all have hot buttons—that is, people, events, and things that upset us. The fourth step in effective emotional management is learning to identify and recognize our triggers ahead of time. This provides us with important opportunities to prepare ourselves mentally and emotionally for those times when someone invariably pushes our buttons. In many cases, it is helpful to visualize the situation or person beforehand. This can help us develop and practice specific strategies for how best to respond, including the beliefs, labels, and self-talk statements that we will use. In the same way that we rehearse mentally for tactical situations, we can prepare for emotionally charged encounters. Taking the time to practice our emotional responses and self-talk is one way of increasing our odds of responding effectively while under pressure.

Improve Emotional Literacy

The fifth step, improving our emotional literacy, focuses on our abilities to recognize and acknowledge specific emotional states. Rather than using the word *anger* to describe every negative emotional experience, we should increase our emotional literacy so that we can more accurately identify and label our feelings. Anger, for example, comes in many forms; a person might be displeased, annoyed, vexed, upset, irritated, agitated, irate, or livid (see Table 6.2). Despite the many subtle distinctions among negative emotions, we often lump them all under one broad category. Because words are powerful, we must be careful with the labels we choose. Although this might seem like splitting hairs, choosing the right word can have a significant impact on how we respond. Telling ourselves that we are angry is more likely to generate hostility than telling ourselves that we are irritated.

Table 6.2 Improving Our Emotional Literacy: Continuum of Labels for Unpleasant Feelings

Annoyed

Irritated

Tense

Uptight

Bothered

Disturbed

Agitated

Mad

Angry

Furious

Fuming

Livid

Outraged

SOURCE: Adapted from Peurifoy, R. Z. (1999). *Anger: Taming the beast.* New York: Kodansha America.

Slow Down the Process

The sixth step is to slow down the process. It should be clear by now that frustration, anger, and other negative emotions can limit our ability to think logically. Strong emotions can drain our mental, physical, and psychological energies, making it difficult for us to concentrate and increasing the likelihood that we will make poor decisions and engage in inappropriate behaviors. Because it often takes time for us to reengage the rational brain, the best way to counter the effects of negative emotions is to increase the time allotted for important decisions or actions. In many cases, simply taking a "time-out" or discussing the best course of action with a coworker can prevent many of the problems and poor choices that often accompany anger.

Reframe

The seventh, and final, step is to change how we think about, or frame, problems and people. How we frame a problem is important because it determines what we look for, how we interpret information, and how we go about solving the problem. Almost any problem can be framed in more than one way. Learning to reframe interactions with difficult people as opportunities for growth can significantly reduce negative emotions or, in some cases, eliminate them altogether. One way of reframing is to change our demands to preferences. We often become emotionally upset when our demands are not met. Because unmet preferences do not usually cause the same level of emotional distress as unmet demands, one way of improving our response is to make a conscious effort to identify and change our demands to preferences.

SUMMARY

Our lives are influenced by two different mental systems: one emotional, the other logical. The two systems—the emotional "go" system and the neutral "no" system—are connected by a collection of nerves that link thinking with feeling. These connections also allow the brain to control events throughout the rest of the body, including the stress response. Most experts agree that there are only two viable options for managing emotions: We can change the environment, or we can change our response. As law enforcement professionals, we are often unable to control our environment. Thus, we must learn to control our responses. Doing so begins with an understanding of the relationship between cognition and emotion, including the importance of beliefs, labels, and self-talk statements. Seven useful strategies for improving emotional management are recognizing the signs, taking responsibility, making a proper appraisal, identifying hot buttons, improving emotional literacy, slowing down the process, and reframing.

The next chapter discusses the sixth, and final, step in the IMPACT model: Take perspective.

STUDY QUESTIONS

1. Anytime we find ourselves overwhelmed with strong emotions, we have two choices. What are they?
2. Explain the three most common myths surrounding anger.
3. Describe the "ABCs" of our emotional responses.
4. How do our beliefs and labels influence our emotional responses?
5. What is self-talk?
6. List five strategies for managing strong emotions.

TAKE PERSPECTIVE

If there is one key to success, it lies in the ability to see things from the other person's perspective.

—Henry Ford

How we see the world has a lot to do with where we stand. Dealing effectively with irate, frustrated, and difficult people has almost nothing to do with "facts." This is because the things that people disagree about usually have less to do with objective reality than with individual perspectives. Whether we are dealing with a frustrated motorist, an irate neighbor, or an angry parent, it is differences in perspective that both define the problem and offer solutions. It is not enough, however, to realize that people differ in their perspectives on the same event. If we want to be truly effective at communicating and connecting with others, we must learn to appreciate their perspectives, with all the power and intensity that go along with them.

Seeing the world from another's point of view is not easy. It requires healthy doses of patience, curiosity, and empathy. Too often, rather than investing the time and energy necessary to fully appreciate other people and their problems, we try to proselytize them to our way of thinking. We assume that if they better understand the "facts," they will see the error of their ways. If, for whatever reason, they fail to "get it," we continue to press our case while ignoring their feelings and their concerns. If they still fail to see the light, we conclude that there must be something wrong with them. Perhaps they are controlling. Perhaps they are stubborn. Perhaps they are ignorant.

Not surprisingly, this approach rarely gets us what we want. Arguing usually does little more than lead to more arguing. Our persistence leads nowhere and nothing is resolved. This is because "facts" are simply one more thing to argue about. Even when everyone agrees, "facts" do little, if anything, to address differences in perspectives and emotions. Our success at communicating and connecting with others depends on our ability to appreciate the perspectives of everyone involved well enough to make sense of them. This makes our ability to take perspective—that is, to step to the other side or to "walk a mile in the other person's shoes"—one of the most important interpersonal skills that any officer can possess.

THE POWER OF PERSPECTIVE

Differences in perception exist because of differences in the ways people experience the world. Our perceptions are shaped by our beliefs, assumptions, goals, values, and expectations. Because no two people share precisely the same beliefs, assumptions, values, and so on, each person experiences the world in a unique way. We all have beliefs about how we should treat others and how they should treat us. We also have beliefs about what is fair and what is just. When we believe that others have treated us fairly, we respond in kind. We are open, receptive, and friendly. Conversely, when we believe that others have treated us unfairly, we become defensive and emotional.

A second reason that perspectives differ from person to person is that we all notice different things. There is simply too much information available to us at any given moment for us to process it all. Inevitably, we must pay attention to certain things and ignore others. Our beliefs, assumptions, and expectations act as filters that influence what we notice, how we respond, and what we remember. The stronger our beliefs or emotions, the more likely we are to select "facts" that best support our self-interests.

It is important to recognize that we can never fully appreciate the complexities of another person's perspective. While we recognize and understand (or at least we think we understand) the experiences, emotions, assumptions, attitudes, and beliefs that shape the way we view the world, the many factors that color others' perspectives are simply too complex for us to grasp. The reverse is equally true: Other people can never fully appreciate the complexities and nuances of our experiences. Invariably, we end up filtering the views of others through our own lenses in ways that produce biased, self-serving conclusions about those others, their behaviors, and their intentions. We often go through entire conversations with other people without realizing that their perspectives and ours are based on different information. Our failure to recognize differences in perspective can stifle our abilities to manage conflict, soothe strong emotions, and persuade others. However, by understanding how we evaluate and explain the behavior of others, we can better appreciate differences in perspective and, in the process, enhance our abilities to connect and to communicate with others.

ATTRIBUTION THEORY

Human beings have a natural need to understand and explain the behavior of others. Indeed, we often spend considerable time thinking about why others behave as they do. Social psychologists refer to the explanations we offer for the behavior of others as attributions. We generally attribute the behavior of others to either internal or external causes. The first kind of explanation, referred to as a dispositional attribution, focuses on internal causes of behavior, such as temperament, personality, and character traits. The cause of the behavior, in other words, resides within the person. The second kind of explanation, known as a situational attribution, emphasizes external causes—that is, factors in the environment beyond the person's control.

If, for example, we merge into a lane of traffic and another motorist responds in a rude or hostile manner, we can attribute that behavior to either internal (dispositional) or external (situational) causes. If we conclude that his behavior is the result of internal factors (personality or character)—for example, "This guy is an idiot" or "What a jerk"—we have made a dispositional attribution. On the other hand, if we decide that his behavior is the product of external factors beyond his control (for instance, he was just fired from his job and is still upset), we have made a situational attribution. The kinds of attributions we make about others, including their motives, intentions, and character, are important because they influence how we interpret and respond to their behaviors.

Because we have a tendency to jump to conclusions while assuming the worst, we need to be careful about the kinds of attributions we make. To complicate matters further, we often respond very differently to the same behavior depending on our attributions. It is one thing for a person who is having an especially bad day to behave rudely, but another thing altogether for a "bad" person to behave rudely. As most of us can testify from experience, we treat "bad" people very differently than we treat "good" people who are simply having a bad day. One problem with dispositional attributions is that the more harshly we judge the other person's character, the easier it is to justify our own bad behavior.

When we make a dispositional attribution, we judge a person's character based on a single incident of behavior. For example, if a person is rude or hostile in one instance, we conclude that she is a "rude" person—that is, behaving rudely or hostilely toward others is part of her character or personality. The same is true of a person who is courteous or polite. We assume that if she acted kindly in one instance, acting kindly is part of her character or personality. Perhaps the greatest problem with dispositional attributions is our tendency to downplay the importance of situational variables (factors beyond the person's control) and to focus instead on the person's character or personality. Indeed, our tendency to look exclusively to dispositional factors to explain the behavior of others is so pervasive that psychologists have labeled this phenomenon the fundamental attribution error.

Despite our natural tendency to offer broad, sweeping indictments of others based on single events, it is virtually impossible to assess a person's character properly based on an isolated incident of behavior. In a famous study on "Good Samaritans," researchers recruited a group of religious seminary students to test the effects of situational and dispositional variables on helping behavior. The subjects first completed personality questionnaires about their religion. Later, they were told to go to another building to continue the experiment. The researchers varied the amount of urgency and the task before sending the subjects to the other building. One task was to prepare a talk about seminary jobs, while the other was to prepare a talk about the story of the Good Samaritan. On the way to the other building, each subject encountered a man slumped in an alleyway whose condition was unknown—similar to the biblical account in the New Testament of a man lying near the roadway in need of help.

In one experimental condition, the subjects were told that they were already late for the task; in the other condition, the subjects were told that they had a few minutes but should get going anyway. As the subjects walked to the other building, they encountered the man in the alleyway, who moaned and coughed twice. Overall, 40% of the subjects offered some help to the man. Much to the researchers' surprise, they found no correlation between religion and helping behavior. Rather, the single most important predictor of whether or not the subjects stopped to render aid was the amount of "hurriedness." In other words, the greater the urgency to arrive at the other building, the less likely the subject was to render assistance. Of all the subjects, those who described themselves as being on a religious "quest" were least likely to render meaningful assistance.

There is little doubt that the subjects in the experiment were good people. Why else would someone choose a life dedicated to helping others? Yet, despite their good character and best intentions, the situational variable of time available, or "hurriedness," had the greatest impact on their decisions to stop and to render assistance. The results of this experiment do not cast doubt on the character of the subjects; rather, they serve as a stark reminder of the powerful effects of situational factors on behavior.

Choice and Intention

The kinds of attributions we make about the behaviors of others are influenced by two factors: choice and intention. To begin with, we are more likely to hold someone responsible for his behavior if we conclude that he chose it freely than if we believe that it was caused by something outside his control (that is, by something in the environment). If someone bumps into us in a crowded market, for example, we are more likely to express anger if we decide the person did so deliberately. The way we evaluate behavior is also influenced by our perception of the person's intentions. If someone hurts us, we are more likely to experience anger if we believe the person did so intentionally than if we determine the harm was unintentional. In the example of the bump in the market, if we fall because the person deliberately pushed us, we are more likely to be angry than if we conclude that the person bumped us accidentally because of factors beyond his control, such as being struck by another person's shopping cart that knocked him off balance.

While we typically blame the behaviors of others on internal factors, we tend to be more generous about our own mistakes. When we are at fault, we are more likely to blame our bad behavior on external, environmental factors than on internal, dispositional factors. If, for example, a motorist cuts into our lane of traffic, we tend to label her discourtesy as part of a larger character flaw or personality deficit. However, if we cut into somebody's lane a few miles down the road, we blame the situation (for example, we had no choice because of heavy traffic).

One reason that we are so quick to blame the behavior of others on internal factors is perspective. The way we observe others is different from the way we observe our own behavior. To begin with, we are aware of the many situational factors that influence our behaviors. To cite the previous example, if we cut into another motorist's lane, we excuse our bad behavior by pointing to heavy traffic and other drivers who refused to allow us the space necessary to merge safely. If the other drivers had been more courteous, we would not have found it necessary to change lanes so abruptly. We also stress the fact that cutting in front of others is not part of our normal driving habits. In other words, we are a "good" person who did a bad thing because of situational factors beyond our control. On the other hand, when we observe the behavior of another person, we know almost nothing about the situation. As a result, we focus exclusively on the person and attribute whatever happens to her personality, character, or other internal factors.

SELF-FULFILLING PROPHECY

We not only try to understand the behaviors of others, but we also try to read their minds. In other words, we try to deduce, based on behavior, what other people are thinking or feeling. One problem with our attempts at mind reading is our tendency to assume that others think, feel, and react in the same ways that we do. We conclude that what is true for us must be true for others as well. The problem is that others often think, feel, and react very differently than we would given the same circumstances. Because we assume that we know more about what others are thinking and feeling than we really do, we fail to watch or listen very carefully. Instead, we act on our assumptions as if they are true.

Despite our best efforts, we are usually not very good at reading others' intentions from their behavior. This is because people's intentions are invisible. Our attempts to read others are further complicated by the fact that intentions—ours as well as theirs—are complex. Sometimes we act with good intentions but do the wrong thing. Other times we act with bad intentions but do the right thing. In still other cases we act with mixed intentions, or we act with no intentions at all—at least none related to the other person.

Our explanations and expectations about the behaviors of others are important because they set the stage for future behavior. One example of the power of expectations is the self-fulfilling prophecy. A self-fulfilling prophecy occurs when our expectations of a person's behavior cause the individual to act in a certain way. If, for example, we smile at someone, he is likely to smile back. If we take a class and expect to learn something, we almost certainly will. If we expect a person to behave rudely or inconsiderately, he will probably not disappoint us.

A self-fulfilling prophecy involves the following four stages:

1. We hold an expectation of behavior for the other person.
2. We treat the person in a way consistent with our expectation.
3. The way we treat the other person causes him to act in a particular way, fulfilling our expectation.
4. The person's behavior reinforces our original expectation.

For example: An officer stops a motorist in an area where residents are known to be hostile toward law enforcement. As the officer approaches the car, he thinks, "Great, another idiot!" Although the officer tries his best to be professional, his voice and nonverbal behavior betray his true feelings. His tone is sarcastic, and he appears irritated by the contact.

The motorist notes the officer's behavior. Predictably, he offers a curt response and little eye contact, and he seems annoyed at the officer's requests. This confirms the officer's original expectation. As the officer returns to his vehicle, he says to himself, "I knew this guy was a jerk!"

The officer's initial encounter with the motorist was strongly influenced by his expectations (stage 1). He expected the motorist to behave rudely, so he treated him accordingly (stage 2). Because of the officer's treatment, the motorist behaved in ways that confirmed the officer's expectation (stage 3). The motorist's rude behavior reinforced the officer's expectation (stage 4).

The self-fulfilling prophecy is one example of how our expectations can shape our encounters with others. Although our expectations do not always result in self-fulfilling prophecies, people do frequently behave in ways consistent with our expectations. In this way, the expectations that we hold of others shape the nature of our interactions. Thus, we need to be careful about the kinds of expectations we form of others, as well as about the verbal and nonverbal messages that we send.

EMPATHY

Empathy is the ability to understand or imagine an experience from another person's perspective. Our ability to empathize is an important part of communicating and connecting with others. It is also an important aspect of managing conflict, soothing hurt feelings, and dealing effectively with irate, frustrated, and difficult people. Our ability to empathize begins early in life. Indeed, young infants can engage in a variety of self-comforting behaviors when exposed to the cries of another child. By 2 years of age, nearly all toddlers engage in some helping behavior in response to the distress of others (emotional empathy). Around the time that children enter elementary school, they already begin to show signs of accurately imagining the perspectives of others (cognitive empathy). Among other things, the development of empathy allows children to offer more effective help to others.

It is important to note that understanding another person's perspective is not the same as agreeing with it. For example, we can empathize with a person addicted to drugs without condoning her behavior.

Similarly, we can understand the anger of a motorist receiving a traffic citation without sanctioning his hostility. Learning to appreciate the perspectives of others is not simply an exercise in helping them feel better; it is a vital skill in every social relationship.

It is always easy to blame others for their "bad" behavior, especially when we conclude that they are unreasonable, ignorant, irrational, or controlling. While it might be easy and, in some cases, natural to blame others, it is usually counterproductive. Rather than helping us to soothe strong emotions, promote positive behavior, and manage conflict, blaming others only makes things worse. None of us responds well to blame, especially when we believe that we have not done anything wrong. By increasing our capacity to empathize, we enhance our abilities to connect with others and to be more persuasive. We can improve our ability to empathize by listening actively, separating problems from people, and acknowledging and validating others' concerns and emotions.

Listen to Be Heard

The first key to empathizing with others is listening. In their book *Becoming a Person of Influence,* authors John C. Maxwell and Jim Dornan suggest, "Instead of putting others in their place, try to put *yourself* in their place" (p. 49). In other words, instead of offering advice or criticism, try to see the situation from the other person's perspective. Advice and criticism only generate resistance. Rather than changing their minds, most people react to criticism by becoming further entrenched in their position. If we want someone to listen to what we have to say, we must first listen to what she has to say. If we want to be heard, we must first allow the other person to be heard. In short, we must take the time to understand the experience from her perspective.

Part of listening effectively is asking the right questions. Unlike advice, proper questions do not criticize or blame. Rather, they allow the person an opportunity to share his story without feeling blamed or criticized. They also provide us with important opportunities to listen, to acknowledge, and to validate the person's feelings and concerns. We are all egocentric to some degree, concerned mostly with our own wants, needs, and fears. As a result, we often treat the concerns of others as unimportant, merely obstacles to be negotiated or ignored. The actual truth of the matter is very different. If we were truly able to experience events in the same ways as the other person, we would probably reach the same conclusions.

While it is important to provide others with opportunities to voice their concerns, simply listening is not always enough. Hurt feelings and unresolved needs do not mend themselves. Before we can communicate, connect, and persuade effectively, we must acknowledge and address the person's emotions and interests, regardless of how unrealistic they may appear to us. Instead of rejecting someone's concerns, invite the person to explain them. We should listen attentively, demonstrate concern, and then reframe the person's story in light of what we have learned. As we have seen, there is more to managing conflict and dealing effectively with difficult people than "just the facts."

Separate Problems From People

The second aspect of empathy is separating problems from people. Every disagreement involves two types of problems: the practical problem and the people problem. The practical problem is the actual person, event, or thing that requires our attention. It is the issue that must be recognized, addressed, and resolved. In contrast, the people problem encompasses the parties involved, including their feelings, concerns, and behaviors. Problems occur when we treat the practical problem and the people problem as one and the same—that is, when we see the person as the problem, not as a person with a problem. When a person is frustrated or rude, we assume that the behavior is part of his personality or character. We seldom look to the situation for an explanation. We fail to recognize that he is frustrated or angry about something or someone. Rather, we simply assume that he is a rude person.

Anytime we fail to separate practical problems from people problems, we risk treating problems and people in the same way. Rather than listening and asking questions, we blame the other person. Rather than trying to understand events from the other's perspective, we jump to conclusions. Rather than remaining open-minded and curious, we assume that the person is stubborn, inconsiderate, or ignorant. We forget that we can be hard on problems yet soft on people. Separating problems from people allows us to look at problems and solutions more objectively and to solve practical problems without unnecessarily damaging relationships.

Acknowledge and Validate

The final strategy for improving our ability to empathize is acknowledgment and validation. One common theme among highly emotional, irate, and angry people is a desire for acknowledgment and validation. The need for recognition appears to be a universal human motivation, and the simple act of acknowledging a person's emotions, interests, and concerns can go a long way toward managing their response. This can be as simple as stating, "So, if I understand you correctly . . ." or "This must be very difficult for you." We all crave acknowledgment and have a strong need to be heard. This is why we continue to press our point until we feel validated. Perhaps the single biggest mistake we can make is advising someone to "calm down" because the problem is "no big deal."

Again, it is worth noting that acknowledgment is not the same thing as agreement. For example, we can acknowledge a person's feelings without condoning his bad behavior or lack of emotional control. Moreover, the simple act of acknowledging a person's concerns and feeling can go a long way toward building rapport, promoting positive behavior, and opening lines of communication.

SUMMARY

How we see and define problems has a lot to do with where we stand. Seeing things from another person's perspective is not always easy. It requires plenty of patience, curiosity, and empathy. However, the ability to see things from the perspectives of others is more than an exercise in helping them feel better; it is critical to the success of every social relationship. One reason people have different perspectives is that we all experience and remember events differently. Because no two people have exactly the same expectations, beliefs, assumptions, values, and needs, no two people experience an event in precisely the same way.

These differences are further complicated by the kinds of attributions we make in explaining our behavior and the behavior of others.

While we typically attribute the behavior of others to internal causes (personality or character), we tend to attribute our own behavior to situational factors (something in the environment beyond our control). This is because we often forget that what we say and do depends as much on situational factors as on personality or character. Our abilities to understand the thoughts, feelings, and behaviors of others depend on empathy—that is, the ability to "walk a mile in someone else's shoes." We can improve our ability to empathize by listening actively, separating problems from people, and offering acknowledgment and validation. Finally, it is important to remember that we can empathize with people without condoning their "bad" behavior or lack of emotional control.

Chapter 8 offers suggestions for improving our communication competence in each of the areas covered in the preceding chapters. This includes discussion of how we can use the Johari window and the conscious competence model of learning to improve our attitudes and skills in virtually every aspect of communication. The final chapter also provides an overview of the importance of assessment, practice, and feedback. While improving our abilities to communicate and to connect with others is often hard work, with the willingness to invest the necessary time and effort, we all can be more successful in establishing rapport, connecting with others, solving problems, managing emotions, and dealing effectively with irate, frustrated, and difficult people.

STUDY QUESTIONS

1. List three reasons our perceptions and perspectives differ from those of others.
2. Describe the two types of attributions we use to understand and explain the behaviors of others.
3. What is the fundamental attribution error?
4. What two factors influence the kinds of attributions we make about others?
5. Explain the concept of the self-fulfilling prophecy.
6. List three strategies that we can use to improve our empathy.

PUTTING THE IMPACT PRINCIPLES TO WORK

———•⋅•———

Model the behavior in your everyday life in a way that always reflects how you would like to be treated.

—Byron Pulsifer

By now it should be clear that everything we do and everything we say communicates important information about our thoughts, feelings, and attitudes. Our posture, mannerisms, facial expressions, eye contact, and choice of words all affect the quality of our interactions with victims, witnesses, subjects, and other members of the public. Our abilities to establish trust, develop rapport, and motivate cooperation all require strong interpersonal skills.

The IMPACT model was developed specifically to provide law enforcement professionals with the skills, knowledge, and attitudes necessary to deal effectively with an assortment of people and a variety of problems across a range of circumstances. Learning to apply the IMPACT principles is part of a four-step process:

1. We must want to change.
2. We must believe in our ability to change.
3. We must learn the necessary skills.
4. We must apply those skills.

The first step in learning anything new is attitude. In order to succeed in any course of self-development, we must honestly want to change. We must see value in changing our current behaviors as well as value in the materials being learned. In some cases, officers might be unaware that they lack good communication skills; in other cases, they may not see the value in learning something new. Unless we believe the new skills will improve our personal and professional lives in some meaningful way, we will lack the necessary attitude and motivation to act any further. As long as we fail to recognize what we do not know, there can be no personal or professional growth.

While the right attitude is critical, attitude by itself is not enough. We must also trust the value of hard work as well as our ability to change. If we believe that communication skills are fixed at birth, there is no reason to act any further. In other words, if we are convinced that good communicators are somehow special or different from the rest of us and that no amount of hard work can change that fact, we see no point in investing our time and energy. On the other hand, if we believe that communication skills can be developed with the right combination of study and practice, we are more likely to invest the resources necessary to succeed. Although certain people seem to be naturally gifted at connecting with others, anyone can improve their communication skills with the right combination of attitude, knowledge, and practice. An officer who is naturally a 4 on a scale of communication ability may never develop his skills to a 10; however, he can improve his skills to a 7 or 8.

The third step in the process is acquiring new skills and knowledge. This requires us to take action—that is, to take specific steps toward gaining the skills and knowledge necessary to become more effective communicators. It is important at this point to identify specific learning resources, including books, courses, and other materials. Reading this book, for example, is an important step toward improved communication skills. It is also useful to set both short- and long-term goals. All goals, however, are not created equal. A goal such as "becoming a more effective communicator" is too fuzzy and too distant to be of any value. Rather, to be of any real help our goals must be specific, measurable, timely, and attainable. For example, we might set a goal to read two books on communication skills in the next three months;

such a goal is specific and measurable (two books), timely (within the next three months), and attainable (the time and resources necessary to meet the goal are available).

The fourth, and final, step in the process is applying our new skills and knowledge. Knowledge itself is of little value without application. Understanding how to communicate more effectively is of no consequence unless it is accompanied by behavioral change. The point of studying and practicing communication skills is to enhance our personal and professional effectiveness. It is only by applying what we have learned that we can discover what works, what does not work, and what we should be doing differently. The more often we use what we have learned, the more comfortable we will become. Improving our communication skills can be a difficult and time-consuming process, even for the most motivated students. It is important to remember that effective communication skills do not develop in a day, but over weeks, months, and years of continued practice.

COMMUNICATION COMPETENCE

Communication competence is a term used by scholars to refer to a person's willingness and ability to communicate so that her messages are understood and she understands others' messages. One of the goals of learning and mastering the IMPACT principles is to increase our communication competence, including our ability to connect with witnesses, victims, subjects, and other members of the public. While the skills and attitudes necessary to communicate effectively can vary depending on the context, one thing is sure: Improving our abilities to communicate and to connect with others requires continuous assessment, practice, and feedback. Without a clear understanding of our strengths, weaknesses, and areas for improvement, we will find it almost impossible to improve our skills in any meaningful way.

Assessment

We acquire many of our communication skills by watching and modeling the behaviors of others. Over time, many of these behaviors become automatic. We no longer think about how to behave; rather, we act out of habit. For example, when we meet a person for the first time, we naturally extend a hand for a handshake. This is because behaviors that are rewarded are more likely to be repeated in the future. While some of these behaviors enhance our interpersonal effectiveness, others can significantly decrease our abilities to communicate and to connect with others. Improving our communication skills begins with an honest assessment of our skills, attitudes, and abilities in all areas of communication by someone we trust. This is especially true of habitual behaviors that operate below the level of conscious awareness.

Practice

The fact that many of our verbal and nonverbal behaviors are rooted in learning helps to explain why people vary so much in their abilities. Indeed, it requires little more than casual observation to discover that some people have more natural communication skills and sensitivity than others. Nonetheless, we can all benefit from regular assessment, practice, and feedback from an expert source, such as an experienced officer who is well versed in communication, patient, and able to articulate her observations. While we should never stray too far from our natural style, understanding how others see us and expanding our range of behaviors allows us to adjust our tone and style to suit the person and the situation.

Feedback

Understanding how others perceive us is an important step in becoming a more effective communicator. We all have habits that limit our interpersonal effectiveness. While we may be consciously aware of some of our bad habits, we may have other habits of which we are completely unaware. Feedback is not only an effective way of identifying areas where we are performing well but also a vital tool for uncovering and correcting bad behaviors. Without honest feedback, we might assume that we have no areas in need of improvement or further development.

To be of greatest benefit, the feedback we receive from others should be timely and specific. That is, the feedback should be delivered as soon as possible after the behavior has been performed, and it should be aimed at particular, measurable behaviors. Abstract or general statements such as "Great job" or "You need to be more positive" are of little value; they are too vague to provide any actual guidance or to identify any specific areas of improvement. Useful feedback is detailed—for example, "You looked toward the ground four different times, kept your arms crossed throughout the entire conversation, and never acknowledged the emotion in his voice." The person receiving such feedback understands clearly the behavioral changes he needs to make to connect more successfully with others in the future.

THE JOHARI WINDOW

We are often unaware of our own behavior and its influence on others. We may have a very limited understanding of even some of our most important actions. Fortunately, there are a number of tools and surveys available to increase our self-awareness and interpersonal competence, including personality and temperament assessments, listening questionnaires, and instruments for identifying conflict style. All of these tools provide potentially valuable information about our strengths and weaknesses in a host of areas. The better we understand ourselves, the better we can tailor our approaches to the unique challenges we face in our personal and professional lives.

The Johari window was developed as a technique for enhancing self-awareness and communication skills. The model is divided into four areas, or quadrants. Each quadrant represents a different level of awareness and provides a unique view of the communicator's style, strengths, and weaknesses, as well as areas of potential improvement. When taken together, the four quadrants represent the total person in relation to other persons.

- *Quadrant 1:* The first quadrant is called the *open* quadrant or the area of free activity. It encompasses behaviors, feelings, attitudes, skills, and motivations known to the self as well as to others. For example, making eye contact during a conversation and shaking a person's hand are Quadrant 1 behaviors. Both the person at whom the behavior is directed and the self are aware of the behavior. The open quadrant varies in size from person to person and is influenced by the individual's openness to experiencing the world. Generally speaking, people vary in their degrees of openness with others and with particular people at different times.

- *Quadrant 2:* The second quadrant is termed the *blind* quadrant. It encompasses behaviors, feelings, attitudes, skills, and motivations known to others but not to the self. This quadrant represents things that others know about us but we do not know about ourselves. All of us have mannerisms, gestures, and idiosyncrasies that we are unaware of until someone brings those behaviors to our attention. For instance, we might be unaware that we look continuously at our watch anytime we speak with a particular coworker, while the coworker is fully aware of the behavior. Because the information in Quadrant 2 is hidden from us but visible to others, it holds the greatest potential to promote our self-improvement.

- *Quadrant 3:* The third quadrant is labeled the *hidden* quadrant. It encompasses behaviors, feelings, attitudes, skills, and motivations known to the self but not to others. This is the area where we hide information about ourselves and about others. In other words, there are things that we know about ourselves but prefer to keep private, as well as information that we know about others but choose not to share. A case in point might be our strong negative feelings toward a supervisor. While we are acutely aware of our feelings, we are able to hide them successfully from our boss. Communicators can choose to keep the material in this quadrant hidden or to make it part of Quadrant 1; such decisions are affected by the nature of the relationships among the parties.

- *Quadrant 4:* The fourth quadrant is characterized as the *unknown* quadrant. It encompasses behaviors, feelings, attitudes, skills, and motivations known neither to the self nor to others. Because information in this quadrant is unknown, there is no way of knowing how a person will respond to certain events until they actually happen. For example, if we have been selected to make a presentation to a large group of people but we have never spoken in public before, we have no way of knowing how we will respond. While preparing for the presentation will certainly help, we cannot know exactly how we will think, feel, or behave until we actually do the presentation.

The Johari window provides a way for us to identify and assess our behaviors in several important areas, including the effects of our behaviors on others. Because everything that we do and say communicates

Figure 8.1   The Johari Window

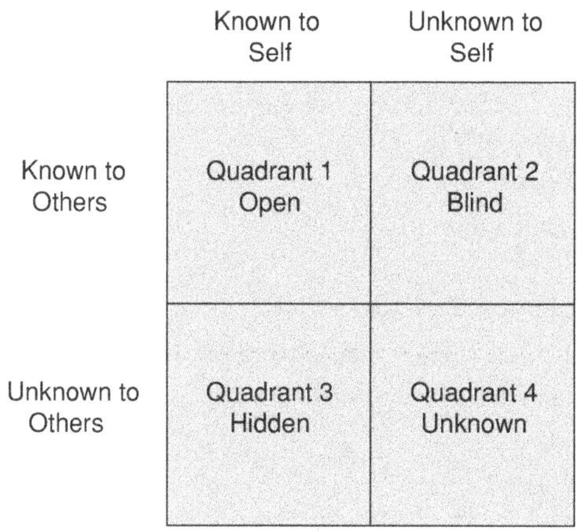

	Known to Self	Unknown to Self
Known to Others	Quadrant 1 Open	Quadrant 2 Blind
Unknown to Others	Quadrant 3 Hidden	Quadrant 4 Unknown

SOURCE: Adapted from Luft, J. (1969). *Of human interaction: The Johari model.* Palo Alto, CA: Mayfield.

something important, identifying and correcting our shortcomings can mean the difference between success and failure in many areas of communication. Because Quadrant 2 behaviors, by their very nature, lie outside our conscious awareness, they hold the greatest potential to promote our self-improvement. While it may be impossible to recognize and modify all of our Quadrant 2 behaviors, we should strive to bring as many behaviors as possible under conscious control. Politicians and others commonly involved in public discourse often allot considerable time to studying how they present themselves, and many spend substantial sums of money on professional coaches to help identify Quadrant 2 behaviors and offer suggestions for improvement. While it may not be necessary to go to such lengths, understanding how others perceive us is an important part of reaching our potential as communicators.

THE CONSCIOUS COMPETENCE MODEL

Learning something new can be a frustrating and time-consuming process. Days, months, or even years may be required to master a new skill fully. The conscious competence model of skill building suggests that we pass through four predictable stages whenever we learn something new:

1. Unconscious incompetence
2. Conscious incompetence
3. Conscious competence
4. Unconscious competence

Several components of this model, including the idea that we are often unaware of what we do not know (unconscious incompetence) are similar to Quadrant 2 of the Johari window.

Unconscious Incompetence

Many officers fail to appreciate the importance of communication. At this stage, officers are unaware of what they do not know. They believe that communicating and connecting with others effectively is reserved for those few officers with the natural "gift of gab." They are unaware of the benefits of communicating with others more effectively, as well as the fact that the skills and attitudes necessary to do so can be learned. Officers at this stage often respond to the challenge of learning communication skills with overconfidence, oversimplification, or complete ignorance that there is a problem or that there is something new to be learned. In any case, officers must recognize their incompetence, as well as the value of communicating more effectively, before they can move to the next level.

Conscious Incompetence

In attempting to deal with an irate, frustrated, or difficult person, an officer often discovers that the person is not responding to the officer's efforts. It is frequently at this point that the officer recognizes the value of learning to communicate more effectively. In other words, the officer is now consciously aware of her lack of knowledge and skills, as well as of her need to learn something new. This is also the time when the officer begins gathering the learning materials and resources necessary to learn to communicate more effectively.

Conscious Competence

At the stage of conscious competence, the officer begins to learn new skills, knowledge, and attitudes. The officer learns to perform new tasks that make it possible to communicate and to connect with others more effectively. While the officer can perform the new behaviors at this stage, doing so typically requires conscious effort and focused attention—that is, the officer must think consciously about what she is doing or not doing. The more the officer practices the new skills, the easier she finds it to use them consistently. Over time and with repeated practice, the officer becomes increasingly comfortable and confident in her abilities.

Unconscious Competence

By the stage of unconscious competence, the officer is able to perform the skills necessary to communicate and to connect with others rather easily, often while simultaneously doing other things. The officer no longer has to think about monitoring her behaviors, listening actively, or identifying emotions; rather, she does so automatically. It is also at this stage that the officer can articulate the skills, knowledge, and attitudes necessary to better communicate and connect with others, as well as to teach others.

Many of the skills outlined in this book may be new to readers (unconscious incompetence). Nonetheless, recognizing what we do not

Figure 8.2   The Conscious Competence Model

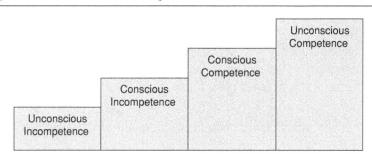

SOURCE: Adapted from Robinson, W. L. (1974). Conscious competency—the mark of a competent instructor. *Personnel Journal, 53,* 538–539.

know, as well as the importance of communicating and connecting with others effectively, represents an important first step in becoming a better communicator. Once we acknowledge the value of learning something new, we can begin to assess our communicative abilities honestly and take steps to improve them (conscious incompetence). When we first apply the IMPACT principles in the field, we will undoubtedly need to make a deliberate effort and devote focused attention to practicing the skills discussed here (conscious competence). While applying our newly acquired skills and attitudes may be uncomfortable at first, with enough time and practice, doing so will become second nature. We will no longer need to think about how best to respond—we will do so effortlessly and automatically (unconscious competence).

It is important to remember that simply wanting to improve our interpersonal effectiveness is not enough. The only way to graduate to unconscious competence is to invest the time, energy, and resources necessary. However, for those officers who make the investment, the payoffs will be substantial. Not only will they be more effective at motivating compliance, managing conflict, and solving problems, but they will also be safer and more effective in virtually every area of the job.

Now that you understand the IMPACT model, don't wait. Begin using what you have learned immediately. Don't expect perfection; rather, aim for progress. To play it safe, start by applying your new skills in situations of low to moderate risk. Celebrate your successes. Analyze what you did right, what you did wrong, and what you can do better next time around. Remember that reaching the level of unconscious competence requires continuous assessment, practice, and feedback. But rest assured that with enough time and practice, you will find yourself applying the principles effortlessly and automatically. When you feel comfortable enough, begin sharing what you have learned with others.

A PLAN FOR IMPROVEMENT

We are all unique in our experiences, expectations, values, goals, and beliefs. Thus, everyone who reads this book will walk away with something different. This section outlines three different plans for how to proceed with what you have learned. Read through all three plans before deciding on a course of action. Because there is no "one size fits all" plan that works for everyone, you should feel free to modify one of the plans to fit your own unique strengths and challenges. You might also find it helpful to combine parts of different plans.

Plan 1: No Progress

After reading this book, if you still find that you have made little progress in your abilities to communicate and to connect with others effectively, remember that simply reading this book is insufficient to promote change. As we have noted, knowledge alone is not enough. To be beneficial, knowledge must be accompanied by behavioral change. You need to apply the IMPACT principles to your personal and professional lives in meaningful ways. While you may be initially uncomfortable, over time and with repeated practice, you will become increasingly skilled. If you still have difficulty practicing what you have learned, you may find it helpful to work with another officer who is especially skilled at communicating and connecting with others. A good mentor can help identify obstacles that might be preventing you from reaching your full potential, as well as offer suggestions for improvement.

Plan 2: Progress, but Desired Results Not Yet Achieved

If you fall into this group, you have probably made good progress in applying the material from the book, but you need additional time and work to achieve the results you desire. To begin with, you may find it helpful to review the materials more than once. Each time you do so, you will gain new insights and abilities. Remember that all of the materials in this book are interconnected, that the total is greater than the sum of the parts. The better you understand the materials at the end of the book, the better you will understand the materials at the beginning, and vice versa. Finally, remember that this book is only a start. Continue along your path of personal and professional growth by reading and studying other materials on communication, conflict resolution, and anger management.

Every book you read and every class you attend will offer new insights and materials that will help you move closer to achieving your goal.

Plan 3: Desired Results Achieved

If you are in this group, you have learned to use the materials in this book so well that you are able to apply your new communication skills automatically and effortlessly. In other words, you have reached the stage of unconscious competence. While this usually requires time and effort, it can be done. Remember, however, that self-improvement is a process, not a destination. There is always something more to learn. Regardless of our level of competence, we can always do better. Don't sit back and admire your work. Rather, continue your course of personal and professional growth by doing supplemental reading, attending courses, and teaching others.

IN CLOSING

It would be naive to suggest that everyone will respond favorably to the approach outlined in this book. Certain people may be too emotional or too controlling to respond to any approach to improving communication skills. Nonetheless, the IMPACT principles have been shown time and time again to be effective with a wide range of people and across a broad spectrum of problems. If using the IMPACT model makes you only 20% more effective, you are now 20% more effective at your job! Even if that translates to nothing more than a single avoided physical confrontation and one less complaint in the next year, you should consider that a success.

It is our abilities to communicate and to connect with others, more than any other skills, that will determine our personal and professional effectiveness. However, we must keep in mind that learning to communicate and to connect with others isn't a destination but a process. Becoming a skilled communicator does not happen in a day; rather, it is something that must be practiced on a daily basis. The more we practice, the better we perform. The only way you can perfect the skills outlined in this book is to keep learning, keep practicing, and keep improving. Remember that the best investment is always in yourself!

STUDY QUESTIONS

1. List the four steps to applying the IMPACT principles successfully.
2. What is communication competence?
3. What are the three strategies we can use to improve our abilities to communicate and to connect with others?
4. Describe the four quadrants of the Johari window.
5. Which quadrant of the Johari window offers the greatest potential to promote our self-improvement?
6. Explain the four stages of the conscious competence model.

BIBLIOGRAPHY AND WORKS CITED

———•••———

CHAPTER 1

Barrett, D. J. (2006). *Leadership communication.* Boston: McGraw-Hill Irwin.

Carnegie, D. (1981). *How to win friends and influence people* (rev. ed.). New York: Pocket Books. (Original work published 1936)

Fitch, B. D., & Means, R. B. (2009). The IMPACT principles: A model of interpersonal communication for law enforcement. *Police Chief, 76*(12), 86–95.

Goleman, D. (1995). *Emotional intelligence: Why it can matter more than IQ.* New York: Bantam Books.

Hebb, D. O. (1949). *The organization of behavior: A neuropsychological theory.* New York: John Wiley.

Infante, D. A., Rancer, A. S., & Womack, D. F. (2003). *Building communication theory* (4th ed.). Long Grove, IL: Waveland Press.

International Association of Chiefs of Police. (2001). *Police use of force in America, 2001.* Alexandria, VA: Author. Retrieved from http://www.cops.usdoj.gov/html/cd_rom/resources_law_enf/pubs/PoliceUseofForcein-America2001.pdf

Miller, T. C., & Zwerdling, D. (2012, March 13). Aftershock: The blast that shook Psycho Platoon. ProPublica. Retrieved from http://www.propublica.org/article/aftershock-the-blast-that-shook-psycho-platoon

Richmond, V. P., & McCroskey, J. C. (2000). *Nonverbal communication in interpersonal relationships* (4th ed.). Boston: Allyn & Bacon.

Watzlawick, P., Beavin, J., & Jackson, D. D. (1967). *Pragmatics of human communication.* New York: W. W. Norton.

CHAPTER 2

Bolton, R. (1979). *People skills: How to assert yourself, listen to others, and resolve conflicts.* New York: Simon & Schuster.

Carter, R. (1999). *Mapping the mind.* Berkeley: University of California Press.

Damasio, A. (2005). *Descartes' error: Emotion, reason, and the human brain.* New York: Penguin Books.

Goleman, D. (1995). *Emotional intelligence: Why it can matter more than IQ.* New York: Bantam Books.

Kagan, J. (1998). *Galen's prophecy: Temperament in human nature.* Boulder, CO: Basic Books.

Lehrer, J. (2009). *How we decide.* New York: Mariner Books.

Loewenstein, G. F., Weber, E. U., Hsee, C. K., & Welch, N. (2001). Risk as feelings. *Psychological Bulletin, 127,* 267–286.

McKay, M., Rogers, P. D., & McKay, J. (1989). *When anger hurts: Quieting the storm.* Oakland, CA: New Harbinger.

Moore, C. W. (2003). *The mediation process: Practical strategies for resolving conflict* (3rd ed.). San Francisco: Jossey-Bass.

Ratey, J. J. (2001). *A user's guide to the brain: Perception, attention, and the four theaters of the brain.* New York: Vintage Books.

Sparrow, T., & Knight, A. (2006). *Applied EI: The importance of attitudes in developing emotional intelligence.* San Francisco: Jossey-Bass.

CHAPTER 3

Adler, R. B., & Proctor, R. F., II. (2007). *Looking out/looking in* (12th ed.). Belmont, CA: Thomson Higher Education.

Adler, R. B., Rosenfeld, L. B., & Towne, N. (1995). *Interplay: The process of interpersonal communication* (6th ed.). Fort Worth, TX: Harcourt Brace College Publishers.

Botelho, R. (2002). *Motivational practice: Promoting healthy habits and self-care of chronic disease.* New York: Guilford Press.

DeVito, J. A. (1986). *The communication handbook: A dictionary.* New York: Harper & Row.

Gottlieb, A., Smith, P., Salovey, P., & D'Andrea, V. J. (1996). Listening skills. In V. J. D'Andrea and P. Salovey (Eds.), *Peer counseling: Skills, ethics, and perspectives* (2nd ed.). Palo Alto, CA: Science and Behavior Books.

Mayer, B. (2000). *The dynamics of conflict resolution: A practitioner's guide.* San Francisco: Jossey-Bass.

Nichols, M. P. (2009). *The lost art of listening: How learning to listen can improve relationships.* New York: Guilford Press.

Nwagbara, U. (2011). Leading by interaction in education organisations: The imperative of leadership communication and complaint management. *Lumina, 22,* 1–20.

CHAPTER 4

Adler, R. B., & Proctor, R. F., II. (2007). *Looking out/looking in* (12th ed.). Belmont, CA: Thomson Higher Education.

Brehm, J. W. (1966). *A theory of psychological reactance.* San Diego, CA: Academic Press.

Cialdini, R. (2001). *Influence: Science and practice.* Boston: Pearson Education.

Cooper, J., Mirabile, R., & Scher, S. J. (2005). Actions and attitudes: The theory of cognitive dissonance. In T. C. Brock and M. C. Green (Eds.), *Persuasion: Psychological insights and perspectives* (2nd ed.). Thousand Oaks, CA: Sage.

Dainton, M., & Zelley, E. D. (2005). *Applying communication theory for professional life: A practical introduction.* Thousand Oaks, CA: Sage.

Franzoi, S. L. (2009). *Social psychology* (5th ed.). New York: McGraw-Hill.

Miller, W. R., & Rollnick, S. (2002). *Motivational interviewing: Preparing people for change* (2nd ed.). New York: Guilford Press.

Peurifoy, R. Z. (1999). *Anger: Taming the beast.* New York: Kodansha America.

Stone, D., Patton, B., & Heen, S. (1999). *Difficult conversations: How to discuss what matters most.* New York: Penguin Books.

Ury, W. (1991). *Getting past no: Negotiating in difficult situations.* New York: Bantam Books.

CHAPTER 5

Brooks, M. (1990). *Instant rapport.* New York: Grand Central.

Carnegie, D. (1981). *How to win friends and influence people.* New York: Pocket Books. (Original work published 1936)

Darwin, C. (1998). *The expression of the emotions in man and animals.* New York: Oxford University Press. (Original work published 1872)

Ekman, P. (2003). *Emotions revealed: Recognizing faces and feelings to improve communication and emotional life.* New York: St. Martin's Griffin.

Fast, J. (1970). *Body language: The essential secrets of nonverbal communication.* New York: MJF Books.

Fitch, B. D. (2010). Selection interviews: The psychology of first impressions. *Police Chief, 77,* 120–126.

Hall, E. T. (1966). *The hidden dimension.* Garden City, NY: Doubleday.

Knapp, M. L., & Hall, J. A. (1997). *Nonverbal communication in human interaction* (4th ed.). Fort Worth, TX: Harcourt Brace College Publishers.

Mayer, B. (2000). *The dynamics of conflict resolution: A practitioner's guide.* San Francisco: Jossey-Bass.

Mehrabian, A. (1972). *Nonverbal communication.* New Brunswick, NJ: Aldine Transaction.

Petty, R. E., & Cacioppo, J. T. (1996). *Attitudes and persuasion: Classic and contemporary approaches.* Boulder, CO: Westview Press.

Richmond, V. P., & McCroskey, J. C. (2000). *Nonverbal behavior in interpersonal relationships* (4th ed.). Boston: Allyn & Bacon.

CHAPTER 6

Clark, L. (1998). *SOS help for emotions: Managing anxiety, anger, and depression.* Bowling Green, KY: Parents Press.

Ellis, A., & Lange, A. (1995). *How to keep people from pushing your buttons.* New York: Citadel Press.

Fitch, B. D. (2009). Emotional intelligence: Practical advice for law enforcement. *Police Chief, 74,* 104–111.

Greenberger, D. A., & Padesky, C. (1995). *Mind over mood: Change the way you feel by changing the way you think.* New York: Guilford Press.

Howard, P. J. (2000). *The owner's manual for the brain: Everyday applications from mind–brain research* (2nd ed.). Austin, TX: Bard Press.

McKay, M., Davis, M., & Fanning, P. (2011). *Thoughts and feelings: Taking control of your moods and your life* (3rd ed.). Oakland, CA: New Harbinger.

McKay, M., Rogers, P. D., & McKay, J. (1989). *When anger hurts: Quieting the storm.* Oakland, CA: New Harbinger.

McMullin, R. E. (2000). *The new handbook of cognitive therapy techniques.* New York: W. W. Norton.

Peurifoy, R. Z. (1999). *Anger: Taming the beast.* New York: Kodansha America.

CHAPTER 7

Crisp, R. J., & Turner, R. N. (2010). *Essential social psychology* (2nd ed.). Thousand Oaks, CA: Sage.

Darley, J. M., & Batson, C. D. (1973). From Jerusalem to Jericho: A study of situational and dispositional variables in helping behavior. *Journal of Personality and Social Psychology, 27,* 100–108.

Eden, D. (1992). Leadership and expectations: Pygmalion and other self-fulfilling prophecies in organizations. *Leadership Quarterly, 3,* 271–305.

Fisher, R., & Ury, W. (1981). *Getting to yes: Negotiating agreement without giving in.* New York: Penguin Books.

Maxwell, J. C., & Dornan, J. (1997). *Becoming a person of influence: How to positively impact the lives of others.* Nashville, TN: Thomas Nelson.

Merton, R. K. (1968). *Social theory and social structure.* New York: Free Press.

Patterson, K., Grenny, J., McMillan, R., & Switzler, A. (2005). *Crucial confrontations: Tools for resolving broken promises, violated expectations, and bad behavior.* New York: McGraw-Hill.

Potter-Efron, R. T. (1998). *Working anger: Preventing and resolving conflict on the job.* Oakland, CA: New Harbinger.

CHAPTER 8

Fitch, B. D. (2014). Communication: The language of leadership. *Law Enforcement Executive Forum, 14*(3), 59–70.

Luft, J. (1969). *Of human interaction: The Johari model.* Palo Alto, CA: Mayfield.

Robinson, W. L. (1974). Conscious competency—the mark of a competent instructor. *Personnel Journal, 53,* 538–539.

INDEX